Informing Transitions in the Early Years

Informing Transitions in the Early Years

Research, policy and practice

Edited by Aline-Wendy Dunlop and Hilary Fabian

Open University Press

Open University Press
McGraw-Hill Education
McGraw-Hill House
Shoppenhangers Road
Maidenhead
Berkshire
England
SL6 2QL

email: enquiries@openup.co.uk
world wide web: www.openup.co.uk

and Two Penn Plaza, New York, NY 10121–2289, USA

First published 2007

A catalogue record of this book is available from the British Library

ISBN 0 335 22013 4 (pb) 0 335 22014 2 (hb)
ISBN 978 0 335 22013 7 (pb) 978 0 335 22014 4 (hb)

Library of Congress Cataloging-in-Publication Data
CIP data applied for

Typeset by YHT Ltd, London
Printed in the Poland byOZGRAF S.A.
www.polskabook.pl

The **McGraw·Hill** Companies

Contents

INTRODUCTION

MODELS OF TRANSITION

CHILDREN EXPERIENCING TRANSITION

PARENTS AND PROFESSIONALS SUPPORTING TRANSITIONS

CONCLUSION

List of contributors

Stig Broström

Stig Broström is associate professor in Early Childhood Education at the Danish University of Education in Copenhagen, Denmark. Since 1969 he has been involved in the field of Early Years Education. Thus, he has much experience in this area, both as pre-school teacher, teacher at a college for pre-school teachers, and as teacher and researcher at the Danish University of Education. His main areas of research are related to children's life in pre-school and kindergarten with focus on children's play, social competence and friendship. His PhD thesis, an ethnographic and comparative study, deals with transition issues exposed through children's social competence and learning motivation in a Danish and American classroom. Currently, he is involved with a research programme that focuses on the development of a curriculum for the early years and reflects the transition theme.

Christine Clarke

Dr Christine Clarke has recently returned to the UK after living and working in Singapore for 13 years. She has been employed as a Specialist Senior Educational Psychologist (Early Years) Pupil and Parent Services, North Yorkshire County Council since May 2005. She previously held the position as Assistant Professor in Early Childhood and Special Needs Education, at the National Institute of Education, Nanyang Technological University for 9 years, where she was involved in training preschool, primary and special school teachers. She has worked in the field of education for 28 years as a teacher, educational psychologist, senior educational psychologist, specialist senior educational psychologist (preschool/early years), teacher educator and researcher. She completed her PhD (Warwick University, UK) in working with parents and children during their final year in preschool and during the transition to primary school. Her specialist fields, both as a practitioner and a researcher, are in the areas of early childhood, early intervention, special needs and working with parents.

Sue Dockett

Sue Dockett is Associate Professor of Education (Early Childhood) at the University of Western Sydney, Australia. Sue started her teaching career in the early years of school and childcare, and has been involved in early childhood teacher education since 1988. Sue's main areas of research are the transition to school—particularly incorporating children's perspectives—children's play and children's thinking. Since 1997, she has been the co-director of the Starting School Research Project, based at the University of Western Sydney. Recent publications out of this project (with Bob Perry) include *Beginning School Together: Sharing Strengths, Starting School: What Matters for Children, Parents and Educators?* and *Transition to School Programs: Development and Evaluation of Guidelines for Best Practice*. Other recent papers include: 'Reading the social landscape: theory of mind and popularity among preschool children' (2003) and 'Young children's views of Australia and Australians' (2003).

Aline-Wendy Dunlop

Professor Aline-Wendy Dunlop has taught in the university sector since 1993: first at Moray House Institute of Education in Edinburgh and from 1996 at the University of Strathclyde where she is Chair of Childhood and Primary Studies in the Department of Childhood and Primary Studies. Until recently she was Course Director of the Certificate, Diploma and Masters in Early Education. She is leading a new PG Diploma route for pairs of nursery and primary teachers who will loop classes during the two years of their course. Aline-Wendy is part of an international team that is developing a European Masters in Early Childhood Education and Care. Her very varied teaching experience over 23 years in schools and the community included home visiting, training education staff in residential childcare, teaching SNNEB students, working with parents, special educational needs and mainstream early education. She is also Lead Director of the National Centre for Autism Studies. Her main areas of current research interest are leadership in early education, special needs, social interaction and understanding in autism, the empowerment of families of very young children, continuity and progression for children in educational transitions and training for professionals in the field of autism. She has been an international research conference chair, is an invited keynote speaker at a range of conferences, and is published both in early education and in autism.

Jóhanna Einarsdóttir

Dr Jóhanna Einarsdóttir is Associate Professor at Iceland University of Education. She received a PhD in Early Childhood Education from University of Illinois in 2000. She has extensive experience in the field of early childhood education. She began as a teacher of young children in 1973 and has been involved in teacher education in Iceland since 1977. She was the director of the Continuing Education department at the College for Preschool Teachers 1989–1996, and division head of the Early Childhood Education department at Iceland University of Education from 1998 to 2001. Her professional interests include early childhood education, early childhood teacher education, and qualitative methodology. She is currently conducting research on early childhood teachers, children's views on their preschool education, and transition and continuity in early childhood education. She has published her work in the United States and in Europe.

Hilary Fabian

Dr Hilary Fabian is Head of Education and Childhood Studies at the North East Wales Institute. She has taught young children in the London Boroughs of Hillingdon and Harrow, in Buckinghamshire, in Shropshire and with the Service Children's Education Authority in Germany. Since 1991, she has worked in the university sector, first at the Manchester Metropolitan University, where she was course leader for the Early Years Continuing Professional Development programmes, then at the University of Edinburgh and, since 2002, at the North East Wales Institute. She has an MSc degree in Education Management, where her dissertation explored staff induction. Her PhD thesis, books and journal publications reflect her interest in educational transitions, particularly children starting school, children transferring between schools and the way in which induction to new settings is managed.

Wilfried Griebel

Wilfried Griebel (Dip Psych) has been working as a member of the scientific staff of the State Institute for Early Childhood Pedagogic and Research, Munich, Germany, since 1982. In his work on family research he has explored children in different family structures. His work on interaction between family and institutions, and especially the studies on transition from family to German kindergarten and from kindergarten to school, undertaken together with Renate Niesel, has given impulses to the development of curricula in

Germany that emphasize coping with transitions. Besides transitions, he works on heterogeneous groups of learners.

Inge Johansson

Inge Johansson is Professor in Pedagogy at the Stockholm Institute of Education. He has more than 25 years' experience as a researcher in the field of linkages and transitions between school, preschool, after-school day-care (fritidshem), and the local community. The main focus of his current research is the development of knowledge and the learning processes in newly integrated school settings, where school, preschool class and after-school day-care are organized as one unit. He has written a number of books, research reports and articles in this field. Inge Johansson has formerly been Research Director for the 'Children, Youth and School' sector in the city of Stockholm and Professor in Pedagogy focused on child research at the University of Linkoping.

Kay Margetts

Kay Margetts is Senior Lecturer in Early Childhood and Primary Teacher Education at the University of Melbourne, Australia. Kay coordinates and teaches across a range of subjects including child development, curriculum, learning and teaching, and professional practice. She has many years experience in the field of early childhood, including professional development of teachers, as a preschool teacher, and writer and producer of children's television programs. Her research interests have a particular focus on issues related to children's transition and adjustment in the early years of schooling. Kay has presented papers at national and international conferences, and has a number of publications. She regularly provides professional development and consultancy to early childhood services and primary schools.

Rosina Merry

Rosina Merry is a lecturer in the Department of Professional Studies in Education at the University of Waikato in Hamilton, New Zealand. She worked in the early childhood sector for a number of years, first as a teacher and then as a director of a large community childcare trust before taking up her position at the University of Waikato. Rosina is currently the National President of Te Tari Puna Ora O Aotearoa New Zealand Childcare Association, a national organization that influences government policies and direction in the area of early childhood education, and has been involved in the development of a range of early childhood legislation and Ministry of Education Research contracts over recent years. Rosina's research interests include transition within early childhood settings, assessment in early childhood and inclusive early childhood education.

Renate Niesel

Renate Niesel (Diplom Psychologin) is working as a member of the scientific staff of the State Institute of Childhood Education and Research in Munich, Germany. She started her work on transitions in the field of family research by understanding divorce as a transitional process demanding complex adaptations and coping strategies from parents and children. Transferring her experience from family research to early childhood education, she carried out empirical studies together with Wilfried Griebel on the transition from family to kindergarten and from kindergarten to school in Bavaria, Germany. She is a member of the State Institute's team developing a curriculum for the education of children in day-care from birth to start of school in Bavaria. Her topics are transitions in the educational system, gender issues and the education of children under three. Besides this, she works as a lecturer for kindergarten and schoolteachers on in-service courses and undergraduate students of early childhood education.

Margaret Parsons

Margaret Parsons had worked in Higher Education since 1998. She is currently Programme Leader for an undergraduate degree course in Primary Education in the School of Education and Lifelong Learning at the University of Sunderland, and teaches Early Childhood and Initial Teacher Education students. Her classroom experience was largely centred on working with children in Key Stage One and she has a particular interest in the learning experiences of children aged 5–6 years. Her main research interests are related to the nature of the early years curriculum, and the provision of appropriate practice in the context of the Foundation Stage and Key Stage One. She is currently involved in a research project focusing on the nature and effects of the transition of children from the Foundation Stage to Key Stage One of the National Curriculum.

Bob Perry

Bob Perry is Associate Professor (Education) at the University of Western Sydney, Australia. Over many years, Bob has combined his academic background and experience in teaching mathematics with research around young children's experiences and expectations. His major research interests include the transition to school, young children and mathematics, teacher beliefs and effective teaching. In his current role at UWS, he is involved in teacher education programmes for indigenous and non-indigenous students. Since 1997, Bob has been the co-director of the Starting School Research Project, based at the University of Western Sydney. Recent publications out of this project (with Sue Dockett) include *Beginning School Together: Sharing Strengths* (2001), *Starting School: What Matters for Children, Parents and Educators?* (1999) and *Transition to School Programs: Development and Evaluation of Guidelines for Best Practice* (2003). Other major papers include 'Mathematics in early childhood education' (2004), 'Early childhood numeracy' (2000) and 'Young children's access to powerful mathematics ideas' (2002).

Margaret Stephenson

Margaret Stephenson is Associate Dean for Education in the School of Education and Lifelong Learning at the University of Sunderland. She has been involved in Early Education since 1976: over a period of 14 years she taught in Nursery, Infant and Primary schools as a classroom teacher and manager of early years provision. She has worked in Higher Education for 14 years teaching Early Years and Initial Teacher Education students. Her research interests are related to the context in which children learn and the development of the reflective practitioner. She is currently involved in a research project focusing on the nature and effects of the transition of children from the Foundation Stage to Key Stage One of the National Curriculum.

Preface

The purpose of this book is to address challenges posed by transitions in early childhood. Challenges exist for practice, for research, and to link research and practice to inform policy development. In this book a group of researchers interested in transitions in early childhood education and care have come together to offer an international perspective on current research, policy and practice in early childhood transitions. We find that there is much in the way of innovative practice, and an increasing body of research evidence that focuses on perspectives of key actors in transitions, and on the process, nature and effects of transitions. The extent to which research and practice are used, or not used, to inform policy development is the greatest challenge of all.

Members of this group have exchanged experience, shared research and developed a concentration of interest in early childhood transition practice over a period of 8 years. We have recognized the need to bring this work more fully to the attention of practitioners, policy makers and fellow researchers, and by so doing to move our own thinking forward further. We introduce our work with definitions of transition that have been embraced or triggered by our research. Each author has provided a short description of the current status of early childhood provision and policy in their own country: although cultural differences emerge, we find there are common themes. These reside in:

- the training and education of practitioners in the field of early childhood;
- the integration or continued separation of care and education services, the age of school start; the relationship between early childhood and later schooling;
- the existence or absence of early childhood national strategies;
- the separation or integration of curriculum and whether curriculum development policy is largely top-down or bottom-up.

At a time when young children are likely to have experienced many different transitions, both educationally and in their family lives, there is an increasing emphasis on an earlier start in group day care and educational settings than ever before. By the time children enter statutory education they may have already attended a number of educational settings. Each of these experiences is likely to affect children and their capacity to adjust and to learn. Such is the significance of early transitions for young children that it is essential that parents, educators, policy makers and politicians pay close attention to young children's experiences in order to provide well for them. Expansion of early education, the nature of the curriculum and the dominance of the 'early start' raise issues of differing perspectives on what is important for young children. Legislation on children's rights demands that children have a chance to express a view; parents have a right of choice in deciding their child's schooling. We explore transitions from different perspectives and ask whether varied perspectives matter, how it is for parents, educators and the children themselves as they move from home to the various educational settings in which they find themselves, how the curriculum can support transitions, and whether there are ways in which policy can better support and empower children in transition?

Each of the countries represented places an increased focus on, and invests considerably in early childhood services. Whether the benefit of this early childhood investment is capitalized on effectively in early primary education, whether transitions can be used as a tool to facilitate this linking of experience and learning for children better, and whether local and national governments are making effective use of the information about transitions that is available to them, are key issues that shape the debate in the final chapter. Here, we introduce a new concept of 'transitions capital'. If children, families and society are to benefit in the longer term from the huge national investment in early childhood services, then government needs to address the links or disjunctions that exist for children as they travel between services, and for their families and the professionals who work with them. We hope that the blend of theory, research and practice included in this book will encourage reflection and help you consider whether present policy addresses transitions for young children appropriately.

Foreword
Janet Moyles

The issue of transitions is one that needs significantly more attention from schools policy makers, practitioners and parents than it currently achieves. There is general acknowledgement that moving from one context to another constitutes important stages in children's lives but the effects on children, parents, schools and settings requires investigation. This is, I believe, what the editors and writers of this book set out to do—and they do it admirably!

As a young child, I remember desperately wanting to go to school. I used to stand with my face pressed against the railings of the local infant school willing someone to invite me in! Yet when I finally started school at almost 5 years of age, the first days were traumatic for me, my parents (neither of whom fully understood what the experiences of the child in school were likely to be), and the teachers. I decided to go home at playtime (imagine the consternation this caused in the school) because, although I desperately wanted to go to school, I didn't want to go all day! What a culture shock! I thought I could go when I wanted to and not as a requirement.

I remember this as just one of the many misunderstandings' inherent in the first few days at school—the other was that, as a competent reader, I was still expected to read the Janet and John schemer, however boring and in-appropriate to my prior knowledge and experiences. Refusal to read this book led to me being kept in at playtime to join the remedial group. My parents could not understand why this avid reader suddenly turned so recalcitrant and reluctant. These are just two examples of hiccups' in a single transition. Probably more difficult and challenging was that having been an only child for the first 5 years of my life, it was extremely difficult to adjust to being one of many – I was obliged to change my whole identity, at least for the time I was in school. What a shame that those trying to support me did not have the benefit of the research presented in this book!

It is refreshing to read about the issues around transitions from such a range of interesting and varied writers and to have a new notion of transitions capital' presented and explored to support future work. The last 15 years or so has heralded a period in time of enormous change for young children and their families. Not so long ago, the majority of children in the United King-dom were raised by parents (and sometimes grandparents) but, on the whole, their first experience of education and care outside the home was their introduction to 'infant school' (Davis 1986). The concept of 'transition', therefore, was a relatively simple one. Children adjusted to school—or didn't—and it was expected that they would settle down as schoolchildren and learn whatever the curriculum provided with little thought to what this meant to them or their parents and carers. It was up to the child to show 'readiness' for school.

Times have changed significantly since then and preschool and nursery settings are well aware of how children and parents are likely to feel when making transitions from home to setting, setting to setting, or setting to reception class. The potential transitions for today's children can be many and varied, even in the course of a single day, and it is vital that practitioners understand the likely effects upon children and parents of such transitions, particularly in the early years. Being a daughter or son, or one of a number of siblings, is very different from being a nursery school child in an institutional setting. Being one of a few children in a childminder setting is equally different. These are just some examples of both horizontal and vertical transitions to which today's young children are exposed.

There is also significant pressure on everyone to achieve an effective early start', for children to settle quickly and to show that they can perform' and achieve educationally and socially according to prescribed curriculum and attainment outcomes. Suddenly, young children are part of the economic society, and transitions need to be effective in many ways, including economically effective, given the investment by national and international governments on ensuring quality' early childhood services.

So what are children's and parents perceptions and expectations about the various transitions they make? The early years is just the start of such transitions, with many others to follow during the years of education, and one could argue that it is vital that we get it right' in the early stages so as to prepare the ground well for children to feel confident with later transitions. Yet effectively the culture and ethos of each setting is likely to be very different, so whatever children learn in one context may be poles apart from their experiences in another and the connections they need to make can feel elusive. Certainly, the culture of school is known to be very different for most children from that of their home experiences or preschool setting experiences (Brooker 2002). Even the 'rules' that govern one situation—like lining up at the door to leave the room—may not apply in another, and this can cause great confusion for a young child and make them feel 'alien' rather than socially comfortable with the situation.

In all transitions one vital element has to be the teachers', practitioners' and parents' skills in understanding how the change affects the individual child. Whilst young children are immensely resilient and resourceful, their reactions to new situations and people and their ability to cope will inevitably be personal. Whilst all young children use their previous experiences to try to make sense of new situations (Donaldson 1992), many will be insufficiently experienced to be able to accept new transitions without significant support from those around them. Many children come from different ethnic groups: their experiences of home and community circumstances may different considerably from those experienced in a preschool or school setting. Even when it comes to play, some children will have had extensive play opportunities and experiences in one context but, because of perceived curriculum pressures, play may be denied in others.

This book emphasizes that there is a dearth of government policies in many countries to deal with transition and continuity issues. Children's voices are rarely sought or heard and yet they are the ones whose self-esteem, confidence and disposition to learning is likely to be most affected. It is also vital that adults who handle and support children's transitions must be on the same wavelength as each other. Communication and sensitivity are vital for ensuring appropriate continuity, as are curriculum expectations which build on a knowledge of children's previous learning experiences and understanding. Practitioners need to act as advocates for children new' to a particular setting whilst at the same time ensuring that they understand how each child feels about and views the transition, and ensure co-constructions of meaning.

This book deals with these and many other issues associated with transitions. It represents the contributors' beliefs and understandings about theoretical, research-based and practical aspects of transitions from an international perspective. The editors are internationally renowned in this field and provide an excellent structure to the chapters. Contributors are extremely knowledgeable about transitions in their own countries and this makes for some immensely valuable and informative comparisons. Readers will be able to draw support, guidance and inspiration from the different writers to scaffold their own thinking and development in relation to children's transitions. The support provided by a book such as this will provide ample opportunities for readers to gain confidence and competence in dealing with the range of people involved in transitions, and benefit everyone, not least the children.

References

Brooker, L. (2002) *Starting School: Young Children Learning Cultures*. Buckingham: Open University Press.

Davis, R. (ed.) (1986) *The Infant School, Past, Present and Future*. London: Bedford Way Papers No.27.

Donaldson, M. (1992) *Human Minds: An Exploration*. Harmondsworth: Penguin.

Acknowledgements

As editors, Aline-Wendy and Hilary would particularly like to acknowledge the authors in this book. To them and to others who participate in this early years transitions network, we extend warm thanks: it is a privilege to work together.

We all extend our thanks to the children, families and practitioners who have participated in our research.

INTRODUCTION

1   Informing transitions

Hilary Fabian

There is an increasing interest in educational transitions because the level of success during transition to school or transfer between phases of education or schools, both socially and academically, can be a critical factor in determining children's future progress and development (Ghaye and Pascal 1989). This opening chapter explores some of the terminology surrounding transition, and seeks to explain some of the differences in transition word-usage between families, practitioners, policy-makers and researchers—'user perspectives'— and the possible meaning and impact of transition for individuals during the transition process. It highlights some of the interconnections between the environment, social contexts, emotional well-being and learning; and raises issues about easing transition, such as the need for informative communication, developing resilience, the changing roles of those involved in a transition, continuity and progression in learning, and the influence of policy.

Underpinning much of the thinking about transitions has been the application of research that explored an ecological concept of transition (Bronfenbrenner 1979), rites of institution, cultural and social capital transfer (Bourdieu, in Webb et al. 2002), cultural understanding and scaffolding (Bruner 1996), and rites of passage (Van Gennep 1960). More recently, the focus on transitions has been on continuity of learning and has included work on pupil mobility (Mott 2002; Strand 2002). Government commissioned studies include transfer between phases of education (Galton et al. 1999; Awdurdod Cymwysterau Cwricwlwm Ac Asesu Cymru (ACCAC) 2004; Office for Standards in Education (OFSTED) 2004; and assessment at transfer Qualification and Curriculum Authority (QCA) 2003). Research that gains children's perspectives and explores children's agency is increasing with the realization that children should have a say in their lives (Thomas 2005) and often look for their own solutions to socio-cultural well-being and curriculum understanding at transfer (Dockett and Perry 1999; Dunlop 2002). For example, Article 12 of the UN Convention on the Rights of the Child (UNICEF) states 'Parties shall assure to the child who is capable of forming his or her own views the right to express those views freely in all matters affecting the child. . .' (http://www.unicef.org/crc/crc.htm).

The chapter concludes by drawing together the broad topics raised by the authors in a conceptual framework, which aims to develop understanding about the complexities of the transition process, and how these could inform the future of research, policy and the practice of transitions.

Times of transitions

In western culture educational transitions take place throughout childhood for the majority of children. For those children who are under three this can include going to a crèche or toddler group, a childminder or group-day-care in nursery, with some children undertaking multiple transitions within a week or even across a day. The main focus of this book is about starting nursery or school, but once at school, transition can become a daily occurrence as children move from Breakfast Club to school to After School Club, albeit on the same site. In Chapter 3 Inge Johansson discusses these vertical and horizontal transitions as processes. He focuses on horizontal transitions that occur throughout the day, which take children between formal and informal situations, and different cultures that necessitate children having to interpret their surroundings and 'read' what is required of them in each setting. He discusses the way in which the social setting influences the learning and the ownership of learning.

As a result of grouping children in ages at school, there is an annual transition of moving from one age group to another, often in a different classroom with a different teacher. The curriculum brings about phase transitions, which often mean a physical move to another school at the same time.

For some children, such as travellers or children of armed forces personnel, transition is a common factor of life (Dobson 2000; Jordan 2000; Ballinger 2001), but for some, transitions are unplanned if parents or children (for example, foster children) move at short notice, either within their own country or, in the case of asylum seekers, to another country. Whatever the circumstances, it is clear that such changes are significant for all children, but especially the most vulnerable such as those with special educational needs or those from dysfunctional families (Napier 2002). Furthermore, such changes take place throughout life, the success of which is often influenced by the first transition.

Terminology

A number of authors (for example, Dockett and Perry 1999; Dunlop 2002; Fabian 2002; Griebel and Niesel 2002; Margetts 2002; Peters 2002) indicate that children, parents and teachers have different perceptions and expectations about what is important during the transition to school. For children and parents it is often surrounded by the excitement of growing up and looking forward to going to 'big' school, where learning becomes more formal. At the end of each year there is a sense of 'moving up' that often involves physically going to another class and another teacher.

Research about transitions increasingly includes perspectives from children and is beginning to explore ways in which children come to terms with change (Einarsdóttir 2003). Listening to those involved in the transition process has begun to add to current understandings of the way in which transition difficulties can be eased (Griebel and Niesel 2002). In Chapter 6, Jóhanna Einarsdóttir highlights children's rights and notes that a Children's Ombudsman has been appointed in Nordic countries to ensure that children's voices are heard. According to the European Network of Ombudsmen for Children there are now at least 23 states in Europe that have ombudsmen or commissioners for children (http://www2.ombudsnet.org/). Einarsdóttir outlines strategies for gathering information from children about their transition at the start of school in a way that acknowledges that children have a right to express their views. In her discussion she draws on examples of children's experiences of starting school from around the world, which recognize that children are experts in, and can have an influence over, their own lives. In the concluding chapter we explore contemporary thinking about consulting with young children and highlight the inherent challenges in such a process.

Practitioners often refer to newly arrived children as the 'new intake' or 'the little ones', and will adopt the technique of 'as if' behaviour (Edwards and Knight 1994), whereby they engage the children in the rules and rituals of the classroom by interacting with them 'as if' they were already aware of the complexities. Settling children into the classroom systems and environment might be enhanced by working collaboratively with parents in order to begin to know about the child's previous learning and plan for curriculum continuity. In Chapter 9, Christine Clarke highlights the importance of communication between practitioners and parents during transitions. She outlines the way in which the system in Singapore is encouraging parental involvement, and empowering parents to become actively involved in understanding their child's transition to school and ways in which they can support their child's learning.

Policy managers are usually concerned with systems such as admissions and the use of assessment across transition phases and the curriculum (QCA 2003). It is then up to practitioners to interpret and implement these in their settings. In England and Wales the introduction of the EYDCPs was seen by some as bringing cohesion to the early years sector and of being supportive to children's transition to school, but they were not necessarily built on genuine partnership and some simply became a mechanism for consultation. In the final chapter, Aline-Wendy Dunlop explores some of the policies that have prompted improvements in transitions and considers how those involved in the transition to school can be influential in bringing about change.

Researchers tend to look at identifying the issues and resolving the problems, particularly of bridging the gaps and making connections for children between settings, both in terms of socio-emotional well-being and learning. Increasingly, the main features of transition are being recognized across a number of disciplines and life stages, and do not just occur within the field of education. There is recognition in the notion of 'crossing borders' that often there are different cultures on either side and, to enable the border to be crossed, those supporting the transitioners need to know the hazards from the learner's point of view and recognize the 'dip' in learning that can occur for many in the transition period (Galton et al. 1999). It is reflection on the research and theoretical understandings that helps to make sense of the research, and uncover the underlying meanings and implications for practice.

The term 'transitions' has no single definition, but is generally understood in educational terms as the *process* of moving from one setting to another, often accompanied by a move from one phase of education to another. It sometimes describes the moves that pupils experience within a school and includes:

- the time between the first visit and settling in;
- a change such as a long-term physical move from one classroom to another during or at the end of a school year;
- a change of teacher during or at the end of a school year;
- the moves that a child makes in any given day between educational settings.

The process of transition is seen as a phase of intensified and accelerated developmental demands that are socially regulated (Fthenakis 1998) and is not complete until the child, once again, is in a state of well-being or feels 'like fish in water' (Bourdieu and Wacquant 1992: 127; Laevers et al. 1997: 15). It is not necessarily linear, but rather a series of interactions where 'the diversity and complexity of transition needs to be valued and understood' (Margetts 2002: 113), and often starts some time before entering a new setting with discussion, planning and preparation. The *induction* period begins with the first pre-visit, and constitutes all the activities and experiences that children may meet during the initial stages of a transition and includes 'all the conditions and processes by which individuals gain direction and encouragement through increased understanding' (Burke 1987: ix).

In much of the literature, the term transitions is used interchangeably with transfer. However, transfer is generally used in the context of the move from one school to another or one phase to another, once full time, statutory education has begun.

In addition to these terms OFSTED (2002) refers to *turbulence*, which is a large-scale planned movement, such as movement following military postings or a school closure, and *transience or trickle factor*, which describes the comings and goings of pupils throughout the school year. These individuals or groups of children moving into or out of a class, either during or at the end of a school year can be a challenge for those children already in the class as they can generate frustration and surprises. In New Zealand, for example, this goes on throughout the year as children begin school on the school day nearest to their fifth birthday.

What does transition mean in practice?

A transition is likely to involve a change of culture and status. It can entail leaving something behind that has constructed an identity (Van Gennep 1960). This could be a place such as home or nursery, or people such as parents or a friendship group (Pollard with Filer 1996). In reality it means leaving the 'comfort zone' and encountering the unknown: a new culture, place, people, roles, rules and identity. The different way of getting to school, the noise, unfamiliar words, new information, teacher's tone of voice, situations such as playtime and lunch time with large groups of unknown people each creates the potential for anxiety, tiredness, discomfort and bewilderment (Barrett 1986; Cleave et al. 1982). However, it can also be seen as an exciting time that involves a number of people working together, and one which children and their parents generally view as a positive one.

In Chapter 7, Sue Dockett and Bob Perry consider issues of continuity and discontinuity that take a broad view of the day, and encompass all the things that happen over a school day, rather than just the planned curriculum. This includes arrival and departure procedures, playground interactions and learning the school culture as part of the curriculum. They explore expectations of children during the school day and the ways in which children manage change.

Entering a new culture

As children enter the next transitional phase they often face a different cultural model from that at home or the previous setting (Brooker 2002). This might include a physical environment that is organized in a different way from the previous setting, differences in the way in which the day is organized, the methods of teaching and the curriculum content, as well as a different social structure. The culture of a setting is central in supporting transitions, and shaping the practice and thinking of transitioners. In order to cope successfully with the demands of school, children have to acquire a range of specific school language and social knowledge, such as the expected ways of behaving. Knowing the rules and knowing what to do is important for children as they start school (Perry et al. 2000), but sometimes children have to 'unlearn' their ways of working in one place in order to adapt to the requirements of the new setting.

Social aspects can be confusing for children when they are expected to work with unknown children in groups chosen by an unfamiliar teacher. More often than not, children are expected to learn the culture, but Bruner (1996) suggests that the culture of the classroom should merge to be a joint creation and that it is 'a complex pursuit of fitting a culture to the needs of its members and of fitting its members and their ways of knowing to the needs of the culture' (Bruner 1996: 43).

When it comes to the philosophical difference between curriculum phases, Margaret Stephenson and Margaret Parsons, in Chapter 10, suggest it causes challenges for all participants, with the potential for loss of continuity in learning for children at a very young age. They contrast the styles of teaching and learning during the transition from the reception class to Key Stage One in England as moving from being actively involved through play in a collaborative environment, to one in which children have a subject-based curriculum and are expected to learn through formal approaches. They suggest that a dip in progression might be the likely outcome of this change.

Changing identity

Changing from being a child to becoming a pupil means mastering the intricacies of the classroom. In order to acquire this new identity, children are expected to behave in a certain way and understand the classroom rules, often without being given instruction. They are expected to learn the language of the classroom and 'read' the teacher, and they are expected to know the way in which teaching and learning are conducted. Sometimes there is a mismatch of expectations between the home and the school that results in confusion and slower progress than expected. For example, Brooker (2005) outlines a case study in which a direct clash of beliefs and practices between parents and teachers meant that, for some children, they became a different kind of child from 'the one their family and community created' (126).

In Chapter 4, Rosina Merry provides an example from New Zealand of the way in which legislation in the curriculum resulted in physical boundaries in a building that constructed different identities for very young children. Teachers then looked for differences in order to provide a developmental rationale for the separation, and to make sense of the boundaries and identities that emerged.

Individual difference

There is immense diversity in development between children from rich and poor families (Penn 2005) which makes each child's transition to school unique (Rimm-Kaufman and Pianta 2000). As a result, adults must recognize that there are a variety of transition experiences for children and cater for individuals within the process. Children commence school with a wide range of personal characteristics, skills, abilities, backgrounds and experiences, but at transition it becomes clear that some children have developed 'emotional literacy' (Goleman 1998) or socio-emotional competence, and are able to cope with change and make sense of school, while others struggle. Those who are coping have developed social competence, resilience and agency that will enable them to transpose their 'symbolic capital' from home to school, 'read' the teacher, make meaning of the nature of school and to deal with new situations. In other words, they are able to function at school and have expectations about learning.

> Given the importance of early school adjustment for later functioning (Belsky and MacKinnon, 1994; Kienig, 2000) it is important to identify children at risk of developmental difficulties so that strategies and practices to prevent or overcome adjustment difficulties and to enhance children's functioning can be implemented as early as possible and preferably prior to the commencement of schooling.
>
> (Margetts 2003: 12)

In Chapter 8, Kay Margetts identifies the difficulties of incorporating individual difference into systems and outlines the implications for transition practice. She explores the influence of gender, temperament, ordinal position in the family, home language, self-awareness, self-regulatory behaviours, academic competence, peer relationships and transition experiences on children's adjustment to aspects of school. Implications for transition practices and policy, including the importance of early identification of children at risk of adjustment difficulties, and strategies for responding to and supporting children's development, are identified.

Supporting transitions

A sense of belonging to the school community contributes to how well children and families adjust (Dockett and Perry 2005). This comes about partly through the relationships between and among children, families and staff, but can also be supported by providing opportunities for social inter-action through grouping children for their learning. Children can be helped to make friends by adults modelling friendship, giving children time to make friends, having buddy systems, introducing children to one another and by using their names so they know who is in the group. Consistent with the findings of Ladd and Price (1987), Margetts (2002: 112) found that children who commenced school with a familiar playmate in the same class 'had higher levels of social skills and academic competence and less problem be-haviours than other children'.

Krovetz (1999) and Goleman (1998) consider that developing social competence such as co-operation and consensus-building, fosters a good start and the ability to cope with change. Winnicott (1974) suggests that bringing a transitional object—a special toy—to school comforts and links the child with other people, especially parents and family, when they are apart. Clearly, there are no simple answers, but practitioners must continue to question their assumptions about their own setting and language, and try to see life from the child's point of view.

One way of supporting transitions is through effective management that uses a variety of communication systems to make the transition meaningful to everyone. According to Margetts (2002), transition programmes are best based on a philosophy that children's adjustment to school is easier when they are familiar with the new situation, parents are informed about the new school, and teachers have information about children's development and previous experiences. In addition, supportive mentoring, co-operation be-tween settings, flexible procedures and evaluation of induction programmes by everyone involved can help to scaffold the process.

In planning effective transition programmes, children's adjustment to a new school environment can be supported through various transitional ac-tivities that create links between and actively involve children, parents, fa-milies, teachers, early childhood services, schools and the local community. These bridging activities value and support continuity of children's previous experiences, relationships, learning and social expectations, and encourage their success. They are a link between phases that help to avoid discontinuity of different pedagogical styles. However, in Chapter 5, Stig Broström suggests that it is not enough just to support transitions through activities; children also need to build a 'mind set' about transitions. In other words, there is a need to build a transition in children's thinking which supports the crossing between philosophical learning boundaries—from play to formal learning. Broström argues that advanced play (frame play or drama play), can mediate between informal and formal systems of learning, and has the potential to influence policies on teaching methods in different phases of education. He outlines a project with children aged 5–8 years, where a 'transitory activity system', was created, which was organized as a series of connected activities: reading of good literature, dialogues on literature, frame play and dialogues with children about their play construction.

Working in partnership

Programmes and practices should be flexible, inclusive and responsive to the local community and its complexity, demonstrating respect for, and acceptance of, diversity and the needs of all those involved. Parents want their child(ren) to be happy and safe and to succeed, so co-constructing transitions with parents in a positive climate—sharing goals, values and expectations— supports transitioners.

In Chapter 2, Renate Niesel and Wilfried Griebel explore the psychological aspects of coping with transitions and the need for effective communication between all participants to enable co-construction of understanding to take place. There are transitions to be made for the child and his/her family, the transition to school being the most prominent one. In the traditionally segmented German educational system that is, crèche, nursery school and school, the main criterion for the allocation of children has been the child's age. However, the need for day care for under-threes and school-children, as well as the introduction of pedagogical initiatives, has promoted a change to a wider age-mix. As a consequence, more heterogeneous groups of learners occur, transitions get less standardized, more flexible and individual, and staff training can no longer specialize in certain age groups. Regarding the transition to school, three microsystems are interconnected in a meso-system: kindergarten staff and peers, school staff and peers, and the child's family (see Fabian and Dunlop 2002). Effective transitions are a function of communication of all participants and of co-construction. Transition competence can be conceptualized as a characteristic not of the child alone, but of his/her social system. Niesel and Griebel address competences concerning the social meso-system of family, nursery school and school in planning transitions and designing curricula, which take into account local conditions and the professional qualifications of staff.

What are the questions for policy-makers?

Policy-makers are those in schools who make decisions about their induction systems, the Local Authorities who regulate admission policies, and government departments that promote policies about the curriculum and wider educational issues. Each of the chapters raises questions for discussion that can be summarized as follows:

- Should there be fewer transitions?
- Should curriculum and age phases that create the need for transitions within the education system be questioned?
- How can institutions be changed to limit transition difficulties?
- How can children be helped to develop resilience and cope with change?
- How can children be given some control and ownership of their transition?
- What is the role of parents in creating procedures that meet their children's needs?
- How does the preparation and initial introduction to the setting reflect all that happens once the child arrives?
- What is the impact of policy from other disciplines upon education policy?

Given the importance of transitions, further questions might be raised about the timing and content of training for staff in early childhood services and the early years of schooling.

In Chapter 11, Aline-Wendy Dunlop develops a discussion about the fusion of policy, practice and research. The potential for the partnership between these different imperatives is considered in terms of psychological, sociological and life course theory. Policy is seen to operate at classroom, school, local and national government levels. With the child's transitions at the centre of the discussion she proposes that transitions are a tool for curriculum and system change. If children are to develop what she calls 'transitions capital' then the day-to-day transition experience needs to be sensitively addressed, informed by research, underpinned by theoretical understanding and assured by policy formulation at all levels.

Summary

This chapter has highlighted some of the challenges that face practitioners and policy-makers, beginning with the amount of transitions that children

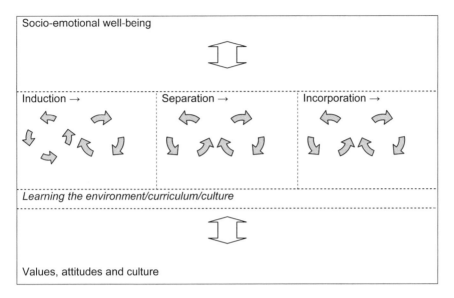

Figure 1. A conceptual framework

undertake in their pupil careers. We define transition as a complex process made up of continued social activity in which the individual lives, and learns to cope, by adapting to the given social conditions. We highlight that children do not learn in isolation, but belong to several microsystems and commute between these environments, adapting to their different demands and learning from each (Bronfenbrenner 1979). These systems are interwoven and on-going, yet transition is often seen as a simple one-off procedure that happens on the first day at a new setting.

We identify what transition might mean in practice as children go through transitional stages (see Figure 1). These stages are cushioned by rituals and ceremonies (rites of passage), which incorporate the child into the group, thereby changing his or her status (Van Gennep 1960). In each setting there is a culture that the child needs to understand to make sense of the new environment. This culture represents the shared values, traditions and beliefs characteristic of the setting, and is informed by the work of Bruner (1996). The recognition of individual differences and ways to incorporate children from a diversity of backgrounds raises questions about how children can be helped to make sense of the changes in their lives, and ways in which parents, pupils and practitioners can work towards shared goals and expectations.

This chapter raises issues for researchers, policy-makers and practitioners about the nature of early educational transition. Children construct evidence and self-perceptions through their own experiences, so building their transition competence depends on their relationships and their circumstances. It is not yet clear if the experience of their first transition influences approaches to future changes. However, it is clear that guided participation (Rogoff 1990) empowers and supports children's attempts to negotiate their way through transitions and become part of their new community of learners.

The theoretical strands bridge sociological and psychological disciplines and are used to build the conceptual framework in Figure 1. This illustrates the reciprocal influence of culture and socio-emotional well-being on the child's learning and progress in the process of being incorporated into the setting. However, the transition process does not always progress in a linear way, but can have periods of no progress or can even regress. This is illustrated by the arrows going in different directions as the child comes to terms with the new environment, the curriculum and culture.

This introduction identifies the chapters in the book that illustrate some of the aspects of transition. The chapters acknowledge the socio-emotional aspects of change that influence learning and can be read individually, sequentially or as part of a group. For example, the first part groups together those chapters that identify the key models of transition such as co-construction, daily change and identities. The second section addresses children's experiences, while the final section draws together chapters that support transition.

References

Awdurdod Cymwysterau Cwricwlwm Ac Asesu Cymru (Qualifications, Curriculum and Assessment Authority for Wales) (2004) *Bridging the Gap*. Cardiff: ACCAC.

Ballinger, A. (2001) *Mobility: Information for teachers and other staff who work with Service Children*. Draft paper presented at the Shropshire Service Schools' Conference: Pupil Mobility: What does it mean?/What can we do? 9 July 2001. Albrighton.

Barrett, G. (1986) *Starting School: An Evaluation of the Experience*. London: Assistant Masters and Mistresses Association.

Belsky, J. and Mackinnon, C. (1994) Transition to school: Developmental trajectories and school experiences, *Early Education and Development*, 5(2):106–19.

Bourdieu, P. & Waquant, L. (1992) An Invitation to Reflexive Sociology. Chicago: University of Chicago Press.

Bronfenbrenner, U. (1979) *The Ecology of Human Development: Experiments by Nature and Design*. Massachusetts: Harvard University Press.

Brooker, L. (2002) *Starting School: Young Children Learning Cultures*. Buckingham: Open University Press.

Brooker, L. (2005) Learning to be a child: Cultural diversity and early years ideology, in N. Yelland (ed.) *Critical Issues in Early Childhood Education*. Maidenhead: Open University Press/McGraw-Hill.

Bruner, J.S. (1996) *The Culture of Education*. Massachusetts: Harvard University Press.

Burke, P.J. (1987) *Teacher Development: Induction, Renewal and Redirection*. Lewes: Falmer Press.

Cleave, S., Jowett, S. and Bate, M. (1982) ... *And So to School: A Study of Continuity from Pre-school to Infant School*. Berkshire: NFER-Nelson.

Dobson, J. (2000) *Pupil Mobility: What, Where and Why?* Paper presented at the Wiltshire County Council 'Smoothing out Turbulence' Conference, 6 July Bradford-on-Avon, Bath.

Dockett, S. and Perry, B. (1999) Starting school: What matters for children, parents and educators? *Australian Early Childhood Association Research in Practice*, 6(3):1–16.

Dockett, S. and Perry, B. (2005) Starting school in Australia is a bit safer, a lot easier and more relaxing: issues for families and children from culturally and linguistically diverse backgrounds. *Early Years*, 25(3):271–81.

Dunlop, A.W. (2002) Perspectives on children as learners in the transition to school, in H. Fabian and A-W. Dunlop (eds) *Transitions in the Early Years: Debating Continuity and Progression for Children in Early Education*. London: RoutledgeFalmer

Edwards, A. and Knight, P. (1994) *Effective Early Years Education*. Buckingham: Open University Press.

Einarsdóttir, J. (2003) When the bell rings we have to go inside: preschool children's views on the primary school. *European Early Childhood Education Research Journal: Themed Monograph: Transitions*, Series 1:35–49.

European Network of Ombudsmen for Children http://www2.ombudsnet.org/ (accessed on 3 November 2005).

Fabian, H. (1999) Small steps to starting school. Key note presentation at *The National Small Schools' Forum Annual Conference*, University of Warwick, 27 March 1999.

Fabian, H. (2002) *Children Starting School*. London: David Fulton Publishers.

Fabian, H. and Dunlop A-W. (eds) (2002) *Transitions in the Early Years*. London: RoultedgeFalmer.

Fthenakis, W.E. (1998) Family transitions and quality in early childhood education, *European Early Childhood Education Research Journal*, 6(1):5–17.

Galton, M., Gray, J. and Rudduck, J. (1999) *The Impact of School Transitions and Transfers on Pupil Progress and Attainment: Research Report RR131*. London: DfEE, HMSO.

Ghaye, A. and Pascal, C. (1989) *Four Year Old Children in Reception Classrooms: Participant Perceptions and Practice*. Worcester: Worcester College of Higher Education.

Goleman, D. (1998) *Working with Emotional Intelligence*. London: Bloomsbury.

Griebel, W. and Niesel, R. (2002) Co-constructing transition into kindergarten and school by children, parents and teachers, in H. Fabian and A-W. Dunlop (eds)

Transitions in the Early Years: Debating Continuity and Progression for Children in Early Education. London: RoutledgeFalmer.

Jordan, E. (2000) *Traveller Pupils and Scottish Schools, Spotlights*, 76. Edinburgh: Scottish Council for Research in Education.

Kienig, A. (2000) 'Transitions in early childhood'. Paper presented at the EECERA 10th European Conference on Quality in Early Childhood Education, London, August 29–September 1, 2000.

Krovetz, M.L. (1999) *Fostering Resiliency*. California: Corwin Press.

Ladd, J. and Price, J. (1987) Predicting children's social and school adjustment following the transition from preschool to kindergarten, *Child Development*, 58(5):1168–89.

Laevers, F., Vandenbussche, Kog, M. and Depondt, L. (1997) *A Process-oriented Child Monitoring System for Young Children*. Leuven: Centre for Experiential Education, Katholieke Universiteit Leuven.

Margetts, K (2002) Transition to school—complexity and diversity, *European Early Childhood Education Research Journal*, 10(2):103–14.

Margetts, K. (2003) Children bring more to school than their backpacks: Starting school down under. *European Early Childhood Education Research Monograph, No. 1: Transitions*, 5–14.

Mott, G. (2002) *Children on the Move: Helping High Mobility Schools and their Pupils*, EMIE Report Number 68. Slough: NFER.

Napier, J. (2002) 'Streets Ahead', *Nursery World*, 102(3818):10–11.

Office for Standards in Education (2002) *Managing Pupil Mobility*, reference number HMI 403, www.ofsted.gov.uk/public/docs2/managingmobility.pdf. (accessed on 5 December 2002).

Office for Standards in Education (2004) *Transition for the Reception Year to Year 1: an evaluation by HMI*, reference number HMI 2221. London: OFSTED.

Penn, H. (2005) *Understanding Early Childhood*. Maidenhead: Open University Press.

Perry, B., Dockett, B. and Howard, P. (2000) Starting school: issues for children, parents and teachers, *Journal of Australian Research in Early Childhood Education*, 7(1):41–53.

Peters, S. (2002) Teachers' perspectives of transition, in H. Fabian and A-W. Dunlop (eds) *Transitions in the Early Years: Debating Continuity and Progression for Children in Early Education*. London: RoutledgeFalmer.

Pollard, A. with Filer, A. (1996) *The Social World of Children's Learning*. London: Cassell.

Qualification and Curriculum Authority (2003) *Foundation Stage Profile*. London QCA/DFES.

Rimm-Kaufman, S.E. and Pianta, R.C. (2000) An ecological perspective on the transition to kindergarten: A theoretical framework to guide empirical research, *Journal of Applied Developmental Psychology*, 21(5):491–511.

Rogoff, B. (1990) *Apprenticeship in Thinking: Cognitive Development in a Social Context*. Oxford: Oxford University Press.

Strand, S. (2002) Pupil mobility, attainment and progress during Key Stage 1: A study in cautious interpretation, *British Educational Research Journal*, 28(1):63–78.

Thomas, N. (2005) The role of a children's commissioner, *Integrate* (the newsletter for the British Association for Early Childhood Education and the Forum for Maintained Nursery Schools and Children's Centres), 4:4.

UNICEF http://www.unicef.org/crc/crc.htm (accessed on 3 December 2005).

Van Gennep, A. (1960) *Rites of Passage* (Translation by M.B. Vizedom and G.L. Caffee) London: Routledge and Kegan Paul.

Webb, J., Schirato, T. and Danaher, G. (2002) *Understanding Bourdieu*. London: Sage Publications.

Winnicott, D.W. (1974) *Playing and Reality*. Harmondsworth: Penguin.

MODELS OF TRANSITION

This first section sets the scene by outlining some models of transition relating to agency, structures and identity. We begin with a traditional model of children starting school, which is recognized by a geographical move from one building to another. In this model, transition can be seen as micro-systems that are interconnected in a social meso-system of family, nursery and school, with parents being of special significance in supporting the child's transition. Communication between all participants and the concept of co-construction are central to bringing about an effective transition, which narrows the gap between the familiar social context of home and the demanding world of school.

The different structures encountered during horizontal transition means that during their everyday life children cross between formal social networks in school and after-school day-care, and also between these formal networks and home. This also represents a transition between various local cultures in the home, school and the after-school day-care. In a world where extended schools are increasing, children are expected to make connections between the different styles of teaching and learning that they encounter in a day and use their abilities to interpret the different ways of behaving in each of these structures.

Children's identity at transition is negotiated between the old and the new, and is influenced by the way in which they perceive themselves. In the case study outlined here from New Zealand, we see that teachers, too, gain an identity connected to the children. In this case, a physical boundary between rooms led teachers to identify the group of children in their care and themselves according to the age of the children with which they worked.

A strong message in this section is that nothing should be taken for granted: transitions across the day, transitions within the same building, and transitions from service-to-service or stage-to-stage, all bring new demands and new opportunities.

2 Enhancing the competence of transition systems through co-construction

Renate Niesel and Wilfried Griebel

Introduction

This chapter deals with psychological aspects of coping with transitions between family and the educational system, focusing on the transition from kindergarten to school in Germany. It aims at improving communication and cooperation of all involved, and tries to enhance the understanding of developmental tasks that children and parents have to cope with. Derived from theoretical work on transitions, transition competence shall be described as a characteristic not of the individual child alone, but a function of communication of all participants (Griebel and Niesel 2003). Children are part of a number of social systems: at transition to school the family, kindergarten and school are each important (Griebel and Niesel 2004a), and have the potential to form a single 'transition system'. For planning transitions, we propose to take into account the competence of this 'transition system'. For professionals of both institutions, it offers a theoretically and empirically founded framework for the conceptualization of transition programmes according to their local context.

Group composition and change

Within a segmented system of child care and education in Germany, children and their families have to cope with numbers of transitions, the transition to school being the most prominent one (Griebel and Niesel 2002). In Germany, crèche and kindergarten (nursery school or preschool) are part of the social welfare system and not of the educational system.

The main criterion for the allocation of children has been the child's age. Traditionally crèche is for children under three, kindergarten for age 3–6 years and elementary school from 6 to 10 years, followed by secondary schools of three different educational levels. As a result of segmentation, homogeneous groups of children are expected and professional staffs are trained for certain age groups. Transitions appear more or less standardized.

Ongoing development of society has led to questioning the homogeneity of such grouping of children in institutional education. One criterion, by which heterogeneity was introduced rather early, is gender. Another changing societal norm in respect to equity has brought about the integration of children with special needs. Group diversity is also reflected in the multi-ethnic or multi-cultural backgrounds of children being educated together. Finally, preschool groups can be heterogeneous by mixed-age versus same-age composition. Variety of age-mix groups in educational settings including day-care and schools is promoted by several factors:

- the need of day-care for under-threes and schoolchildren after school hours;
- experiments with more flexibility concerning the age of school entry;
- a new emphasis on early childhood education, in general, and pedagogical initiatives focusing on a broader age mix, in particular (Griebel et al. 2004).

Heterogeneous groups of children reflect heterogeneous families: families differ in the number of children, their age and gender and whether they have children with special needs; families also have different ethnic and cultural backgrounds. Families are also different in respect to their experiences of transitions in their family development, for example, divorce, remarriage or migration (Fthenakis 1998).

Where groups become more heterogeneous, demands on staff training are changing, and transitions require a more differentiating and individualized perspective.

Transition to school as topic of international research

Entry into the system of formal schooling has been a topic of great interest in international early childhood research. There are studies from many countries in Northern Europe, from Australia, New Zealand (www.extranet.edfac.unimelb.edu.au/LED/tec), and Singapore, from the US and from Canada (Griebel and Niesel 2004b). As a background to these studies, no matter how different the systems of institutional education, school entry has turned out to be a significant developmental step for the child and her/his family. Transition causes stress. About one-third to one-half of new school children show behaviour that has been described as adaptation problems, developmental disharmonies or transition reactions. Creating continuity between educational contexts before and within school traditionally seems to be the leading paradigm to solve transition problems. On the other hand, coping with discontinuities stimulates development of the child and her/his family and cannot be avoided. Therefore, competencies for coping with discontinuity will be a central question for future research on transition to school.

Factors that influence transition

An array of factors has been examined that influence the child's transition to school. Apart from characteristics of the child, such as a positive attitude in respect to school and learning (Entwisle and Alexander 1998), and social competencies (Margetts 2002), there are factors on an interactional level, such as parents' positive attitude towards school and learning, friends of the child going to the same classroom and a positive child–teacher relationship (Pianta 1999). Information from school, transition activities on the part of the school, communication between school and family before the child enters school are all important on a contextual level. A better communication between practitioners in the preschool setting and school teachers, and co-operation of preschool, school, parents and community has been found to foster effective transition to school (Pianta and Kraft-Sayre 2003). For socially disadvantaged children a high quality preschool program is especially important. Where there are ethnic/lingual minorities, it has been proved that fit between the cultural background of children and the capacity of schools to meet diversity is important for the transition to school (Yeboah 2002).

A theoretical concept of transition

Transitions are a complex field of theory and research, dealing with processes of change in the life context. Transitions are characterized by phases of concentrated learning and accelerated development in a social context (Welzer 1993). Bronfenbrenner (1979) defined a child's entry into an educational institution as an ecological transition. Commuting between family setting as the primary developmental context and school setting as a secondary developmental context, demands adjustment and brings about changes in identity, relations and roles. Adaptation to new demands has been studied within the stress paradigm. Theories on stress (Lazarus and Folkman 1987), as well as on critical life events (Filipp 1995), consider the appraisal of the critical event as being important. It is not the event itself, but the coping process that makes it a transition. Development over the life-span takes into consideration, that not only the development of the child, but also of her/his parents is stimulated through a transition. From a background of family developmental theory, Cowan's (1991) concept of family transition is adaptable to the multiple demands concerning transitions between the family and the educational system. In order to understand and support individuals' and families' adaptation to changes, Havighurst's (1956) concept of developmental tasks, more generalized by Oerter (1995), seems useful. In a socioconstructivist perspective, transition is a process of co-construction through communication and participation between institution and family (Griebel and Niesel 2002). In a comprehensive theoretical model, these different approaches are taken into account. The transition model includes a family perspective. Parents support their child's transition and undergo a transition themselves to being parent of a school child. Staff members in early childhood institutions and in school co-construct the transition, but do not cope with developmental tasks for themselves (Griebel and Niesel 2004a,b).

Transition from kindergarten to school is a developmental task

For children and parents, transition leads to changes on an individual level, on an interactive level and on a contextual level. These changes mean discontinuities in the child's and the family's experiences.

Developmental tasks on the individual level

The transition from kindergarten to school means changes of identity—being a school child is different from being a child in kindergarten. Strong emotions like excited anticipation, curiosity and pride, as well as insecurity and fear have to be coped with. New competencies like growing independence, and new skills opening the world of reading and writing are expressions of developmental progress.

Developmental tasks on the interactive level

Building of new relationships with teachers and new classmates has to be accomplished. Existing relationships undergo changes, some will end, for example, with kindergarten teachers and kindergarten friends. Relationships within the family change as well. Expectations and sanctions concerning the role of being a school child differ from a kindergarten child's role. This means the child has to fulfil a new role additional to his/her role in the family.

Developmental tasks on the contextual level

The main task is the integration of the demands of two different settings: school and family, with the school's schedule determining the family's organization of the day, the week and the year. Learning has to follow school curriculum instead of pedagogical approaches typical for kindergartens. If other transitions within the family (such as the birth of a sibling, parent returning to work, and so on) take place close to school entry, transition to school may become more complicated.

School readiness, increasing heterogeneity in classrooms and the necessity of co-construction

In the academic discourse in Germany the understanding of school readiness has changed substantially in the last years (Kammermeyer 2001). Reasons are to be found in the unreliability of standardized assessment methods (Mandl and Krapp 1978) and the growing scientific knowledge on the complexity of transition demands. Nickel (1992), referring to Bronfenbrenner (1979), developed an eco-systemic model of school readiness that integrates the child, as well as the micro-systems of family, kindergarten and school into an interacting meso-system. Then school readiness is no longer to be seen as a child's status at a certain point of time, in the sense of a cumulative skill model. Rather school readiness has to be regarded as an objective and a common responsibility of child, family, kindergarten and school, thus pointing to co-construction processes. Becoming a school child can only happen if the child gets a chance to experience school life. This implies that there is no conceptualization of school readiness that is suitable as a selection criterion for decisions about which child may go to school and which child may not. Researchers even plead for an end of school readiness discussions and the abolition of this construct (Kammermeyer 2001) as the question 'Is this child ready for school?' has to be completed by the question 'Is this school ready for this child?'. Nevertheless, school readiness remains a crucial point in the transition from kindergarten to school, for parents, as well as for teachers, especially as the age range of school entrants is widened and practitioners have to find an answer.

School readiness is a good example for the necessity of mutual clarification of expectations and the understanding of learning and education of preschool teachers, school teachers and family members. This is emphasized by the increasing heterogeneity of school beginners and their families' perspective. Co-construction has been proposed as an approach to integrate people and perspectives because the transition to school is a developmental demand which may accentuate disparities.

In a co-constructive approach, the participants try to clarify how the processes of learning in different settings (home, kindergarten and school) can be interconnected and thus optimized, following the principle that a child's knowledge and expertise shall not be devalued at the beginning of formal schooling, but further developed. McNaughton (2001) addresses the problem with regard to literacy practices of families having different ethnic background in New Zealand. He proposes the co-construction of parents' and teachers' expertise by finding out what the ideas about school readiness and literacy practices held by parents and teachers are, and how they can be related to each other in order to enhance the learning processes of the child. Kammermeyer (2001) in Germany studied the differences between kindergarten teachers and school teachers regarding their assumed features of school readiness. The mutual clarification of subjective theories (Kammermeyer 2001) of professionals is one important aspect that allows the linking of learning processes between kindergarten and school. Conclusions from these studies are that efforts to enhance transition for children need to consider the ideas about learning and education that socialization agents hold. The participation of the child him/herself is an additional problem.

Parents are always implicated in education, either as silent, passive partners or as vocal, active partners. Traditional approaches of family involvement with much emphasis on involving parents in ways that address the school's agenda, prescribing traditional roles for parents, such as volunteering or homework helper have been successful for children of middle-class families, where there is continuity between the needs, beliefs and knowledge about education of school and families. Christenson (1999) proposes a partnership approach to family involvement instead. Partnership approach is characterized by a belief in shared responsibility for education and socializing children. Although both families and educators have legitimate roles and responsibilities, the emphasis is not on the roles families can play for schools. Rather, the emphasis is on relationships: specifically, how families and educators work together to promote the academic and social development of children.

To consider and value backgrounds of children and families that differ from societal mainstream can be understood as 'diversity awareness' (McNaughton 2001). It is a professional competence that has to be developed further. According to Pianta et al. (1999) the development of supportive family–school relationships should not be considered a correlate or antecedent, but rather an outcome of school transition.

The necessity for linking a child's learning in different settings through processes of co-construction leads to the question of the competence or effectiveness of the child's social system.

Transition competence as competence of the social system

In respect to transition to school, and to a transition systems approach (Dunlop and Fabian 2002: 146), three micro-systems are interconnected in a meso-system: the child and their family, the kindergarten staff and organization, and the school staff and organization.

Within each of these micro-systems that co-construct school-readiness, the question for competences to do so arises.

Heterogeneous families have to deal with...

Families differ in respect to the competencies they hold to cope with the transition to being a family with a school child. Within the family, some individual competencies of the child that are relevant for the transition to school child have been investigated empirically. Examples are self-esteem and emotional well-being (Fabian 2002), social skills including cooperation, assertion, responsibility, empathy and self-control (Margetts 2002), and pre-academic competencies like literacy (Makin 2003).

To illustrate the idea of differing competencies of the family as a social system, three models from family developmental psychology shall be taken into consideration: attachment quality, adaptability and family coping.

Development of a child's secure attachment is a result of the match of the child's attachment system and an adult's nurturing behaviour. Attachment theory has become the rationale for a standard procedure for the transition of children under three and their parents into child care institutions. Secure relationships with their institutional caregivers shall be established so the child can build a secure base for exploring and further educational processes (Beller 2002). Not only the child, but also the parents are active participants in this process, well prepared and instructed, and in ongoing exchange with the professional caregivers. The transition procedure from family to crèche therefore is based on the competence of the social system child–family child care institution. Different educational outcomes can be expected from different attachment styles within the social system.

A scheme for classification of family relationships and family competencies has been proposed as the Circumplex Model of family by Olson et al. (1989). The model contains the dimensions of cohesion and adaptability. Adaptability means the capacity of a family system to adapt to situative and developmental demands and changes. Different styles of adaptive ways of reorganization of power structure, role relations and rules have been classified. The model has become a stimulus for systemic assessment and treatment of families.

As a part of family stress theory, dyadic coping has been introduced by Bodenmann (1997). This view of stress in close relationships—partnerships—implies a person–environment systemic perspective. Experience of stress and coping are related to the dyad (or group). Different styles of dyadic coping could be identified as being functional (for example, common coping, supportive coping) or dysfunctional (for example, ambivalent coping, hostile dyadic coping). The concept of dyadic coping has been transferred to wider interpersonal contexts, that is, to the family (Laux et al. 2001). Consequences for prevention of stress and for family intervention have been drawn.

...two different worlds of learning culture (and vice versa)

Within the microsystems of early childhood educational institutions (in Germany: kindergarten) and school, social skills, as well as professional qualification are important individual competencies of members of staff.

Cooperation between kindergarten and schools is difficult if there is a lack of administrative coordination, a difference in professional understanding of education of learning culture and professional culture, and if communication problems with the family about education learning, play and achievement exist (Neuman 2002). Strategies in European countries to optimize cooperation between the early childhood educational institutions and school can be found on three levels: curricula development, administration and personnel interaction (Oberhuemer 2004a,b). Therefore, cooperation on these three levels shall be seen as competencies of the social system.

On the level of curricula, there is a need of fit between programs in both institutions. This is a political matter especially where different ministries and administrations are responsible for early childhood education and for school. Practically, staff in kindergarten enhances children's basic and pre-academic competencies, and supports the transition readiness of the child to school-child. In current development of curricula for kindergartens in Bavaria, the topic transitions and especially transition to school has been integrated (StMAS and IFP 2006); the same will happen in Hesse in 2007.

Staff in school continues the education of children and supports transition to school by transition activities. Agreement between kindergarten and elementary school on common educational objectives has to be achieved for basic competencies, for example, a positive self-image, self-confidence and learning how to learn. Promoting literacy and numeracy in both educational settings also has to be a topic of cooperation. This does not only mean to prepare children for the school's requirements, but also that schools value pedagogical input from kindergarten and promote the further development of basic competencies. The prevailing strategy to enhance a better fit on the curriculum level can be described as establishing more continuity.

On the level of administration, there is a need to combine responsibilities better for child education throughout the child's development and by establishing transitional programmes (Margetts 2002). This is a special challenge in Germany's segmented educational system. Structural means of regular cooperation have to be installed. Furthermore, a common education, and achieving equal working conditions for practitioners and teachers, would promote professional cooperation. Cooperation with parents also is a topic that is very relevant for transition to school. Competence of the social system links here to the quality of the regular cooperation structure between practitioners, school teachers, and parents.

. . . an example for a local culture of cooperation

In Germany, compulsory school starts at about age 6 years, and the school year starts in mid September. On the day of inscription to elementary school, around Easter 2004, in Hassfurt, Bavaria, there arose a question about a 5-year-old boy. He knew letters and counted numbers, and to the practitioners in kindergarten, he seemed to be intellectually ready for school. However, he appeared to be rather shy, and needed social and emotional support so that he would meet new challenges. He would have been of school-going age, if he had been born before June 30. His birthday was August 4 and he could go to school if the parents wished him to do so. His father supported the transition to school right away for him to get enough intellectual stimulation; his mother would prefer him to wait for another year to stabilize him socially and emotionally. The parents, the educators of the kindergarten and a school teacher with advisory function had a meeting about what the family, the kindergarten and the school could do to make the boy ready for school within 4 months. They decided to offer more opportunities for meeting new children in new contexts that would stimulate him to express himself. He started to join the second group in his kindergarten for an excursion and special occasions as well as a junior club for sports. These activities should confront him with different social situations and purposes, but less for intellectual stimulation. Parents and educators kept monitoring his social behaviour and development. After 4 months—including some family holidays—everybody considered him ready for transition to school, and there he was. His new teacher agreed to monitor his participation in class activities.

Conclusion

As increasing heterogeneity of school beginners and their families in a changing society has been identified in the last decades, demands on staffs in kindergarten and schools are changing. Transition then require a more differentiating and individualized perspective as the transition to school is a developmental demand at which disparities begin to appear.

Co-construction has been proposed as an approach to integrate people and perspectives, involving communication, cooperation and participation between families, educational institutions, and children. It is a way in which the individual needs of all children in heterogeneous groups can be met, linking a child's learning in different settings. On the level of personnel interaction, obligatory models of long-sighted (continuous) communication and cooperation can be combined with ongoing professional qualification. Development of (preschool) curricula can be seen as a means of support of communication and cooperation leading to co-construction between professionals in preschool and school, as well as with parents.

References

Bayerisches Staatsministerium für Arbeit und Sozialordnung, Familie und Frauen and Staatsinstitut für Frühpädagogik (2006) *Der Bayerische Bildungs- und Erziehungsplan für Kinder in Tageseinrichtungen bis zur Einschulung. Offiziell über. arbeitcte Fassung.* Weinheim: Beltz.

Beller, K. (2002) Eingewöhnung in die Krippe. Ein Modell zur Unterstützung der aktiven Auseinandersetzung aller Beteiligten mit Veränderungsstress, *Frühe Kindheit*, 5, 2, S. 9–14.

Bodenmann, G. (1997) Dyadisches coping: Theoretischer und empirischer Stand, *Zeitschrift für Familienforschung* 9, S. 25.

Bronfenbrenner, U. (1979) The ecology of human development, *Annals of Child Development*. Cambridge: Harvard University Press.

Christenson, S.L. (1999) Families and schools: rights, responsibilities, resources and relationships, in R. C. Pianta and M. J. Cox (eds) *The Transition to Kindergarten*. Baltimore: Paul H. Brookes.

Cowan, P. (1991) Individual and family life transitions: A proposal for a new definition, in P. Cowan and E. M. Hetherington (eds) *Family Transitions: Advances in Family Research*. Hillsdale: Lawrence Erlbaum.

Dunlop, A-W. and Fabian, H. (2002) Conclusions: Debating transitions, continuity and progression in the early years, in H. Fabian and A-W. Dunlop (eds) *Transitions in the Early Years. Debating Continuity and Progression for Children in Early Education*. London: RoutledgeFalmer.

Entwisle, D.R. and Alexander, K.L. (1998) Faciliating the transition to first grade: the nature of transition and research on factors affecting it, *Elementary School Journal*, 98(4): 351–64.

Fabian, H. (2002) Empowering children for transitions, in: H. Fabian and A-W. Dunlop (eds) *Transitions in the Early Years. Debating Continuity and Progression for Children in Early Education*. London: RoutledgeFalmer.

Filipp, H-S. (1995) Ein allgemeines Modell für die Analyse kritischer Lebensereignisse, in H-S. Filipp (ed.) *Kritische Lebensereignisse*. Aufl. Weinheim: Beltz.

Fthenakis, W.E. (1998) Family transitions and quality in early childhood education. *European Early Childhood Education Research Journal*, 6(1): 5–17.

Griebel, W. and Niesel, R. (2002) Co-constructing transition into kindergarten and school by children, parents, and teachers, in H. Fabian and A-W. Dunlop (eds) *Transitions in the Early Years. Debating Continuity and Progression for Children in Early Education*. London: RoutledgeFalmer.

Griebel, W. and Niesel, R. (2003) Successful transitions: Social competencies pave the way into kindergarten and school, *European Early Childhood Education and Research Journal, Themed Monograph No.1, Transitions*, 25–33.

Griebel, W. and Niesel, R. (2004a) Transition competence of the child's social system. Poster presented at the *14th Annual Conference on Quality on Early Childhood Education, Quality curricula: the influence of research, policy, and practice*, Malta, 1–4 September, 2004.

Griebel, W. and Niesel, R. (2004b) *Transitionen. Fähigkeit von Kindern in Tageseinrichtungen fördern, Veränderungen erfolgreich zu bewältigen*. Weinheim: Beltz.

Griebel, W., Niesel, R., Reidelhuber, A. and Minsel, B. (2004) *Erweiterte Altersmischung in Kita und Schule*. München: Don Bosco.

Havighurst, R.J. (1956) Research on the developmental task concept, *School Review. A Journal of Secondary Education*, 64: 215–23.

Kammermeyer, G. (2001) Schulfähigkeit: In: Gabriele Faust-Siehl; Angelika Speck-Hamdan (Hrsg.). *Schulanfang ohne Umwege* (S. 96–118). Frankfurt/M.: Grundschulverband—Arbeitskreis Grundschule e.V.

Laux, L., Schütz, A., Burda-Viering, M., Limmer, R., Renner, K.-H., Trapp, W., Vogel, S. & Weiss, H. (2001) *Stressbewältigung und Wohlbefinden in der Familie*. Stuttgart: Kohlhammer. 2. erw. Aufl.

Lazarus, R.S. and Folkman, S. (1987) Transactional theory and research on emotions and coping. *European Journal of Personality* 1: 141–70.

Makin, L. (2003) Literacy prior to school: Narratives of access and exclusion. *EECERJ* 11(1): 93–103.

Mandl, H. and Krapp, A. (1978) Diskussionsebenen für eine Neuorientierung der Schuleingangsdiagnose. *Neue Modelle, Annahmen und Befunde, Göttingen*, S. 9–28.

Margetts, K. (2002) Planning transition programmes, in H. Fabian and A-W. Dunlop (eds) *Transitions in the Early Years. Debating Continuity and Progression for Children in Early Education*. London: RoutledgeFalmer.

McNaughton, S. (2001) Co-constructing expertise: The development of parents' and teachers' ideas about literacy practises and the transition to school, *Journal of Early Childhood Literacy*, 19(1): 40–58.

Neuman, M.J. (2002) The wider context: An international overview of transition issues, in H. Fabian and A-W. Dunlop (eds) *Transitions in the Early Years*. London: RoutledgeFalmer.

Nickel, H. (1992) Die Einschulung als pädagogisch-psychologische Herausforderung—'Schulreife' aus ökosystemischer Sicht, in D. Haarmann (ed.) *Handbuch Grundschule. Band 1.* Weinheim: Beltz.

Oberhuemer, P. (2004a) übergang in die Pflichtschule: Reformstrategien in Europa, in D. Diskowski and E. Hammes-Di Bernardo (eds) *Lernkulturen und Bildungsstandards: Kindergarten und Schule zwischen Vielfalt und Verbindlichkeit.* Jahrbuch 9 des Pestalozzi-Fröbel-Verbandes. Baltmannsweiler: Schneider-Verlag Hohengehren.

Oberhuemer, P. (2004b) Bildungskonzepte für die frühen Jahre in internationaler Perspektive, in W. E. Fthenakis and P. Oberhuemer (eds). *Frühpädagogik international. Bildungsqualität im Blickpunkt.* Wiesbaden: Verlag für Sozialwissenschaften.

Oerter, R. (1995). Kultur, Ökologie und Entwicklung, in R. Oerter and L. Montada (eds) *Entwicklungspsychologie.* Weinheim: Beltz (3. Aufl.).

Olson, D.H., Russell, C.S. and Sprenkle, D.H. (1989) *Circumplex Model: Systemic Assessment and Treatment of Families.* New York: Haworth.

Pianta, R.C. (1999) *Enhancing Relationships Between Children and Teachers.* Washington, DC: American Psychological Association.

Pianta, R.C. and Kraft-Sayre, M. (2003) *Successful Kindergarten Transition.* Baltimore: Brooks.

Pianta, R.C., Rimm-Kaufman, S.E. and Cox, M.J. (1999) Introduction: An ecological approach to kindergarten transition, in R.C. Pianta and M.J. Cox (eds) *The Transition to Kindergarten.* Baltimore: Paul H. Brookes.

Speck-Hamdan, A. (2004) Anschlussfähigkeit sichern—über institutionelle Grenzen hinweg. *KiTa aktuell BY*, Nr.10: S. 198–202.

StMAS and IFP (2006) vol. 6 *Bayerisches Staatsministerium für Arbeit und Sozialordnung, Familie und Frauen and Staatsinstitut für Frühpädagogik.*

Welzer, H. (1993) *Transitionen. Zur Sozialpsychologie biographischer Wandlungsprozesse.* Tübingen: edition discord.

Yeboah, D.A. (2002) Enhancing transition from early childhood phase into primary education: evidence from the research literature. *Early Years*, 22: 51–68.

3 Horizontal transitions: what can it mean for children in the early school years?

Inge Johansson

Introduction

The meaning of transition for children, and the impact of it for their development and socialization has become an important area for study during recent years. Focus has very much been on the early years, the period when the children literally and physically move from preschool to school. Leaving one arena, with its specific social and cultural code, and moving into another one with a different set of values and ways of constructing meaning about what is important in the surrounding world is a complex and complicated process for most children. Each setting has its own structure with formal, as well as informal developmental tasks for the child. They must learn how to adjust to the local code in the setting they enter and learn successful ways to relate to others there. Each child must generally go through such transitions. It is important to understand transition in relation to what happens to a child when she or he leaves one service and its setting and comes to another. What does the first setting mean for the child and how do the experiences there affect the experiences in the other one? In this chapter I will discuss the transition concept and emphasize horizontal transitions as an important area for further studies. This is done with an illustration from a study on how children experience school, home and after-school day-care.

What is transition?

What is meant by transition is wide and, in many cases, not very well defined. Fabian (2004) has made a penetrating effort to define the concept and its various meanings. She says that transition describes the moves that pupils experience in a school. Such moves include:

- the time between the first visit and settling in;
- a change such as a long-term physical move from one physical locality to another during, or at the end of, a school year;
- change of teacher(s) during a school year;
- a change of children such as a group of children moving into or out of the class during a period.

All this can change the situation for a child or a group of children in a way that we can talk about as transition. While these situations vary, Fthenakis (1998) suggests that transitions can be periods of intensified and accelerated developmental change, influenced by social situations and contexts involving the environment, social and cognitive learning, as well as emotional turmoil. Transitions usually involve transitioners changing roles, status and identity. Transition also means a change in social relations and dynamics in the group with which a child is involved. Relationships between children/ adults and children/children affects the ability to settle quickly.

Two American researchers (Kagan and Neuman 1998) have analysed the content of the transition concept in a meta-study of three decades of transition research. They found three main interpretations of the concept. One regards transition as one-time activities undertaken by children, families and programmes at the end of the year. Another regards transition as an ongoing effort to create linkages between children's natural and support environments (that is, linking families to programmes, children to their communities). A third group regard transition as the manifestation of the developmental principle of continuity (for example, creating pedagogical, curricular and/or disciplinary approaches that transcend and continue between programmes). From this, transitions are defined as the continuity of experiences that children have between periods and between spheres of their lives (Zigler and Kagan 1982).

Transitions affect children in many ways including their own learning and development, and their relationship with their socio-cultural context at different times. The dynamic nature of what constitutes transition, as I see it, is that it is more relevant to talk about a transition process or transition processes, rather than single actions or occasions.

The direction of the transition processes

An established way to identify and obtain better understanding of the ingredients of the transition process is to sort them by their temporal dimensions. Here, we can talk about vertical and horizontal transition processes, respectively (Kagan 1991). The best known of these are the vertical transitions that deal with moves and changes for the child between educational settings such as preschool or school, but also inside school between the grades and various teachers (Griebel and Niesel 2002; Broström 2001; Peters 2002). Vertical transitions are clearly linked to the children's increasing age and the related environmental changes.

Horizontal transitions involve children's transition during their everyday lives between formal social networks in school and after-school day-care, and between these formal networks and home. These types of transitions often involve frequent changes between settings within relatively short time frames.

Horizontal transition

Horizontal transitions are a part of modern-day life for young children. In many countries, many children go from home to school and back again, often with intermediate stops for various recreational activities, such as soccer practice, dance lessons and so on. During recent years it has become increasingly the case that young children go from home to school, then to an after-school day-care programme and home again. This development is especially significant during the first school years. The Nordic countries, for example Denmark and Sweden, have a long tradition of such autonomous services (fritidshem) for young children. These services have their own pedagogical tradition with specially educated staff, and goals that combine care and education. The overall majority of Danish and Swedish children attend such a service during their first 2–3 years in school. In many other countries such as England, Scotland and Germany there is a strong trend toward such programmes for young children after school (Cohen et al. 2004). This means that many, in some countries most, of the children meet with at least two different social systems beside their informal social network (family and peers) during an ordinary school day. The complexity for the child to adjust to and interpret the surrounding world has in this respect increased.

A socio-cultural, ecological and relational perspective

To understand horizontal transitions better, the home, school and after-school day-care can be seen as systems that are highly influenced by the social and cultural conditions in society at a given time. They can be seen as systems that interact with each other in a dynamic way and, in this respect, construct meaning for the child (and other people, too) by the relations and symbols that become significant for interactions across the day.

The term culture refers to thriving patterns of natural behaviour, routines, ways of apprehending the surrounding world and interpretations of what is going on, that have grown over a long period. Culture includes in this sense, common knowledge, values and experiences that form uniting patterns of thinking and interpretations. Culture is the frame inside which individuals form themselves in a myriad of social relations (Säljö 1999). The social system in which the child is included does not operate independently from the others and, therefore, the interrelatedness of children's school, home and after-school day-care settings each need to be considered. In such an ecological approach (Bronfenbrenner 1989) it is possible to contend that children, parents and teachers co-construct transitions in the context of their overlapping experiences and the cultures in which they live (Dunlop 2003). The social relations, values and norms in each setting form a pattern that can be seen as a micro-system. The interconnections between these settings are as important to the child as the events taking place within each individual setting (Bronfenbrenner 1989). In this perspective, it is important to underline that within the micro-system the transition concept has no implicit value. Neither does it say anything about the quality of its constituent actions. Transition though, has much in it that affects the child and their situation, and this is represented by the interconnection of the meso-system (Fabian 2004). Thus, it is inside the socio-cultural and ecological frame that the individual child forms, and is formed by, relationships by interpreting and acting upon significant symbols and gestures (Mead 1934).

In such a dynamic perspective, linking macro- to micro-levels, horizontal transition takes form and affects the child. As pedagogy and process is of vital interest here, the meaning of the transitions for the child focuses on learning.

The social and situation-related dimension of learning

For children's learning all situations and peer-relations are of vital importance. Such processes for meaning and learning have been studied together and discussed as a major part of the day-care pedagogy (Williams et al. 2000). Learning goes on between individual and group discourses and cultures. Such a perspective means that learning cannot be avoided in interacting on a micro-, as well as the macro-level (Säljö 1996, 2000; Williams 2001). The interesting aspect is how learning affects the individual, and how knowledge can be seen in actions and ways of thinking. What mainly directs the content of the learning are the situations and the social climate where the new knowledge is formed.

Situated learning theorists such as, for example, Lave and Wenger (1991) argue that learning is social and contextual. Learning happens in and is bound by specific shared social practices. Learning is situated in the specific environment in which it takes place. In this view learning is about shared social knowledge and skills appropriated, or constructed, in and related to, shared social practice (Broström 2003). Pedagogical processes of children learning together and from each other, have not been studied in the horizontal transition from school to after-school day-care before. Experience of such processes comes mainly from the preschool (Williams et al. 2000). Children aged between 6 and 9 years, the ages when they normally go to the after-school day-care have, in most cases, developed the ability to understand each other's perspective. In Piagetian terms their thinking has reached a level of decentration. Many aspects in the after-school day-care stimulate the children's communicative ability. The children must continuously communicate to solve practical problems and conflicts, exchange information, negotiate rules, and so on. Lev Vygotsky (1982) points to children incorporating the communicative process itself when they are experiencing the interplay with peers, and thereby create building tools for their thinking. In this way, the cognitive development goes on and the child's understanding of the surrounding world expands. Results from research (Damon 1984) show that peer-collaboration facilitates the development of empathy, kindness and a sense of justice. Learning together stimulates and includes not least the social and emotional dimension for a person in relation to others. This has also been verified by a Swedish study (Williams 2001), which found that older children could help the younger ones intellectually and in relation to conflict-solving. The children saw each other as resources where the young children asked the older ones and learned from them. Another aspect that affects the child's experience of horizontal transitions is the extent to which knowledge from one setting is useful and applicable in another.

The conclusion from this is that children learn from each other in a dynamic and independent way by active and mutual participation in everyday activities. It is easy to see this as an idealistic view including many positive aspects, but it can also lead to quite the opposite result. Children can learn to oppress each other and marginalize another child in a group. A child can sometimes have difficulties using knowledge learned in one setting, in another setting with a different culture and social practice.

How do children in the early school years experience settings for horizontal transitions? Some results from a Swedish study

In a Swedish study a group of 12 children, six girls and six boys in two after-school day-care centres (fritidshem) were followed during a 3-year period. The main purpose of the study was to investigate how the children experience the content of the everyday life in the after-school day-care (Johansson 2004; Johansson and Ljusberg 2004). Since 1998 the school in Sweden has included a special class for the six-year-olds, called the preschool class. The main purpose for the preschool class is to facilitate the transition from preschool to school. Six-year-olds typically attend a preschool class in the morning and after-school day-care after lunch.

The following section reports a comparison of children's understandings of the different settings. The perspectives of girls are reported first, followed by the responses of the boys involved in this study. The focus of the descriptions is on the preschool/after-school day-care or on the after-school day-care/home transition.

The girls

Mary (one of the girls) says that the preschool class is a place for the children to learn the competencies they need in order to begin school. This means such things as to learn to behave properly, listen to the grown-ups and speak to them in a friendly manner so they do not become irritated and in a bad mood. Brigitte identified significant differences between the preschool class and school. In the preschool class it was mostly 'circle time and pottering' she says. In school there is more defined work, homework and scheduled activities. In the after-school day-care the main activity is play, the girls say. The after-school day-care is a place for play and the school is a place for work with various subjects. In the after-school day care we learn how to act in a proper way to each other, she says. Sometimes when she is at home she thinks of what she is doing in the after-school day-care. If she has been busy and engaged with something there she looks forward to going there again as soon as possible.

When Christine tells about the after-school day-care she stresses three things that are important. The first thing is that there are many children to play with. The second is that the children are usually allowed to do want they want themselves and the third thing is that the staff are kind to the children.

The main difference between the after-school day-care and the home is that at home you are allowed to do whatever you want, Brigitte says. There are fewer children in the home setting and there are also less out-door activities to do when you are at home. Brigitte does different things at home compared with the other setting. For example, two of her main interests at home are to care for her rabbit and ride her horse. Christine says that she would rather be in the after-school day-care than at home because there are so many more children to play with there. She often thinks of the after-school day-care when she is with her parents.

The responses of the girls indicate that attending the after-school day-care is fun and the girls are comfortable there. The main difference to school is that in the after-school day-care you are allowed to play, in school you are not.

Christine explains it like this.

I: If you compare the school and the after-school day-care?

C: Yes, then the after-school day-care is by all means the best. Because in the classroom we must sit still the whole time, listen, listen, sit, sit, look, look, write, write, read, read. In the after-school day-care we could play as much as we wanted to, besides when we were called to circle time and had to go out.

However, if she had the opportunity of taking her friends home she thinks that could be even better. That is because at home she can do precisely what she wants, she says—even take out the dolls to the garden, which she was never allowed to do in the after-school day-care. Karen agrees with this.

Elsie explains her choice between being at home and in the after-school day-care, like this.

I: If you could choose between being at home and going to the after-school day-care?

E: The after-school day-care!

I: Why?

E: Because we have much more fun there, more fun than in school and when I am at home.

Karen says that you learn different things in school compared with the after-school day-care. She says:

You learn to have fun there, you learn things, and you learn to play games.

All the girls report that they are comfortable in the after-school day-care, and to a certain extent also in the preschool class and in school. Their stories are much about the freedom to do as they want: a freedom they are very satisfied with. Such freedom is much less in the school setting, but even more at home, compared with the after-school day-care.

The boys

All the boys say that they like being in the after-school day-care. However, two of the boys, Marcus and Sam thought that it is even better to be at home. At home, Marcus says you get new toys regularly and in the after-school day-care you are not allowed to go outside the park. It is in that sense more restricted than at home. By contrast, George thinks that it is sad to go home at night because there are more children and toys in the after-school day-care. Initially, he says that he does not learn anything in the after-school day-care, but on second thought he says that they learn to write in an artistic way there.

When George compares school and after-school day-care he is more comfortable in after-school day-care because he can play with new things there all time, and he likes that the best.

In the after-school day-care you learn to be a good friend, the boys say. Sam likes school the least. In school you are not allowed to play, he reports. All you can do there is to sit still and be silent, and that is not fun. Sam explains that he must go to the after-school day-care because his parents are at work and no one is at home to take care of him. He shows insight about what the after-school day-care is for. In school he says, you learn a lot, but in the after-school day-care hardly anything. The good thing is the freedom there to do whatever you want. Marcus agrees with this. If he could choose freely, he would be at home.

All the boys indicate that the after-school day-care means freedom to do what they want, but it is the grown-ups that have the main responsibility for what is going on there. They also report that the grown-ups have the power and are the ones that make most of the decisions for the whole group.

A difference between home and after-school day-care is that you do not have to go out so much when you are home, Nick says.

The responses from the boys fit in with what we saw previously from the girls. John would prefer to be at home if he had the choice. He says.

> I: If you could choose between to be at home or in the after-school day-care what would you do?
> J: Be at home.
> I: What is better being at home then?
> J: One can do more of what you really want to do there.

Some of the boys say that they tell their parents about what they are doing in the after-school day-care, other say they never do. I tell them only if I am asked, John says. Then he says that it is fun there and talks about the games they play.

Discussion

The after-school day-care is a unique setting for the children where they spend a substantial part of their day away from home. They experience it as significantly different from the other settings in which they spend their everyday life. All children, in our study perceive clear differences between how it is being in school, at home and in the after-school day-care. Generally, the answers from the children show that they experience the after-school day-care as providing much more freedom for them compared with school.

In the after-school day-care the general opinion of the children in the study is that they can do things that they cannot do at home, and there are also more activities and choices for them there. In school, the focus is on work and learning, while the after-school day-care promotes play, and provides much more free time to spend with peers and doing things together.

There are distinct differences between home and after-school day-care. At home the children have more individual freedom to do what they want. However, there are more options in the after-school day-care, more toys, games and opportunities to do things together.

Compared with school and its structured teaching, the after-school day-care is much freer. These differences are summarized like this by a girl:

> The difference (compared with school) is that you do not have to work in the after-school day-care, but that you have to do this in school. There you must sit on a chair and listen to the others. The good thing about after-school day-care is that you can play there and you cannot do that in school.

The integration, between school and after-school day-care, which has taken parts of the same organization and literally placed them under the same roof, has meant few real changes in the content and structures of each service. The children have no difficulties in separating them and identifying what characterizes each of them.

The after-school day-care is basically a place for play. The best quality in this is the amount of children. The individual can choose from several ongoing activities and take the initiative for new activities with others.

Previous research from the preschool sector has shown that the children themselves separate play and learning (Pramling Samuelsson and Asplund Carlsson 2003). The children in this study connected the school work to formal learning. When they had time to reflect on what they do in the after-school day-care many of them said that they also learn in this setting. However, compared with school they learn other things there. They learn to be a good friend, respect each other, cooperate and so on. These are aspects that can be seen as social and informal learning. This shows an understanding of learning that is not always considered. In this respect, it is important to take notice of what the children describe when they talk about what they are doing. Such descriptions do not always have a meaning that fits the concepts that have been established in the world of the grown-ups and in the mainstream culture. The most obvious example here is the meaning of learning. When the children themselves get the opportunity to describe the content of what they are doing and reflect on it, they are able to see other dimensions in what is happening and look at learning from a wider perspective.

The rules and regulations for social relations between the children, and between the grown-ups and other children in the after-school day-care are constructed and reconstructed from one time to the next by ongoing negotiations and a struggle for power. Such open social systems as the after-school day-care and the home also include space for actions and negotiations that can lead to compromises, winners and losers. The implication of the social system for such negotiations has been studied by some British researchers (Mayall 1996; Wyness 1999). They found that the children were more successful in their social actions in the home compared with school and can challenge the power of the grown-ups. Children have more negotiating power in settings that are socially open and less formalized. In this respect a main quality in the after-school day-care is that it gives more space for the children's own actions and initiatives, and this helps them to increase their power to participate and take an active part in play and games from a democratic perspective. The children are empowered when they can form rules, and see and feel that they can influence what is going on and take responsibility for it. Obviously, children experience differences between the formal educational settings in school and after-school day-care. They see different aspects of quality between being at home, in school and in the after-school day-care. Their comparisons of these settings leads us to gain more knowledge about what the horizontal transition between these three main social systems means for children's socialization and construction of meaning of their surrounding world.

The interplay between horizontal and vertical transition processes

Horizontal and vertical transitions are two processes that occur simultaneously, but can also conflict with the other. The transitions, both the horizontal and the vertical are highly affected by the relations between them, and how homogenous or heterogeneous they are. On the official level both kinds of transition processes aim to facilitate by integration, involving a team of teachers with various competencies, who are responsible for the child during the whole day in school and after-school day-care. In a study of the practical content of what happened when an integrated approach was developed during the period in school, Nilsson (2004) concludes that encounters between culturally diverse educational institutions are difficult. To have tools for such integration that really support transition, it is necessary for the pedagogues, preschool teachers, school teachers and recreational pedagogues (fritidspedagoger) involved to reflect on their cultural, and pedagogical history and tradition. On the basis of such reflections an integrated and cooperative approach can be established so that the environment in the school is more homogenous and thus better for children's transitions. This indicates the need for future studies critically analysing public goals for transitions in relation to practice. What do we know about what is really happening in transition processes and what that means for the children?

One important question in this respect is what the transition means for children's learning. The conclusion is that transition, in general, and well-functioning transitions, in particular, facilitate children's social learning. Establishing schools with a wider brief and responsibility to encompass the community, as is beginning to occur in many countries, means educational settings with a greater complexity, including programmes for social development and care. This new way of defining what is included in school and ambitions to develop connections to surrounding social networks, informal, as well as formal ones, highlights the importance for gaining knowledge and further understanding of what is included in horizontal transition processes and the interrelationship between horizontal and vertical transition processes.

References

Bronfenbrenner, U. (1989) Ecological systems theory, in R. Vasta (ed.) *Six Theories of Child Development Revised Formulations and Current Issues*. London: Penn.

Broström. S. (2001) *Farvel börnehave- hej skole! Undersögelser og overvejelser. (Bye-bye kindergarten—Hello School! Research and Reflections)*. Systime. Århus.

Broström S. (2003) Transition from kindergarten to school in Denmark, in S. Broström and J. T. Wagner (eds) *Early Childhood Education in Five Nordic Countries*. Systime. Århus.

Cohen, B., Moss, P., Petrie, P. and Wallace, J. (2004) *A New Deal for Children. Reforming Education and Care in England, Scotland and Sweden*. Bristol: Policy Press University of Bristol.

Damon, W. (1984) Peer education. The untapped potential. *Journal of Applied Developmental Psychology*, 5:331–43.

Dunlop, A-W. (2003) Bridging early educational transitions in learning through children's agency, *European Early Childhood Research Journal*, Monograph Series No. 1:67–86.

Fabian, H. (2004) Defining transitions. Poster presented at the *European Early Childhood Research Association*, 14th Annual Conference, Malta, September 2004.

Fthenakis, W.E. (1998) Family transitions and quality in early childhood education, *European Early Childhood Education Research Journal*, 6:5–17.

Griebel, W. and Niesel, R. (2002) Co-constructing transition into kindergarten and school by children, parents and teachers, in H. Fabian and A-W. Dunlop (eds) *Transitions in the Early Years Debating Continuity and Progression for Children in Early Education*. London: RoutledgeFalmer.

Johansson. I. (2004) To learn and to get together. Paper presented at *European Early Childhood Research Association* 14th Annual Conference, Malta, September 2004.

Johansson, I. and Ljusberg, A-L. (2004) *Barn i fritidshem (Children in after-school day-*

care centre), Individ omvärld och lärande/Forskning nr. 21. Lärarhögskolan i Stockholm. Stockholm.

Kagan, S.L. (1991) Moving from here to there. Rethinking continuity and transitions in early care and education, in B. Spodek and O. Saracho (eds) *Yearbook in Early Childhood Education* 2:132–51. New York: Teachers College Press.

Kagan, S.L. and Neuman, M.J. (1998) Lessons from three decades of transition research. *Elementary School Journal* 98(4):365–80.

Lave, J. and Wenger, E. (1991) *Situated Learning*. Cambridge: Cambridge University Press.

Mayall, B. (1996) *Children, Health and Social Order*. Buckingham: Open University Press.

Mead, G.H. (1934) *Mind, Self and Society*. Chicago: University of Chicago Press.

Nilsson, M. (2004) Transition as Integration. Paper presented at the AERA conference, San Diego, 12–16 April 2004.

Peters. S. (2002) Teachers perspectives of transition, in H. Fabian and A-W. Dunlop (eds) *Transitions in the Early Years Debating Continuity and Progression for Children in Early Education*. London: RoutledgeFalmer.

Pramling Samuelsson, I. and Asplund Carlsson, M. (2003) *Det lekande lärande barnet i en utvecklingspedagogisk teori* (*The Playing, Learning Child in a Developmental Pedagogical Theory*). Stockholm: Liber.

Säljö, R. (1996) Samtal som kunskapsform (Conversation as knowledge-form), in C. Brusling and G. Strömqvist (eds) *Reflektion och praktik i läraryrket*. Lund: Studentlitteratur.

Säljö, R. (1999) Kommunikation som arena för handling- lärande i ett diskursivt perspektiv. (Communication as arena for acting—learning in a discursive perspective), in C.A. Säfström and I. Östman (eds) *Textanalys*. Lund: Studentlitteratur.

Säljö, R. (2000) *Lärande i praktiken. Ett sociokulturellt perspektiv* (*Learning in Practice. A Socio-cultural Perspective*). Stockholm: Prisma.

Vygotsky, L. (1982) *Taenkning og sprog* (*Thought and Language*). Köpenhamn: Hans Rietzel.

Williams, P., Sheridan, S. and Pramling Samuelsson, I. (2000) *Barns samlärande. En kunskapsöversikt* (*Children Learning Together*). Stockholm: Skolverket. Liber.

Williams, P. (2001) *Barn lär av varandra. Samlärande i förskola och skola* (*Children Learning From Each Other. Learning Together in Preschool and School*), Göteborg Studies in Educational Sciences, 163. Göteborg Göteborgs Universitet.

Wyness, M. (1999) Childhood, agency and educational reform, *Childhood* 6(3):353–68.

Zigler, E. and Kagan, S.L. (1982) Child development knowledge and educational practice, in A. Liberman and M. McLaughlin (eds) *Policy Making in Education. Eighty-first Yearbook of the National Society for Study of Education*. Chicago: University of Chicago Press.

4 The construction of different identities within an early childhood centre: a case study

Rosina Merry

(Adapted from an article published in 'The First Years Nga Ttau Tuatahi', *New Zealand Journal of Infant and Toddler Education, 2004, 6(1))*

Introduction

This research, in an early childhood centre in Aotearoa New Zealand, explores aspects of transition from an 'under-two' programme to an 'over-two' programme in a childcare centre. The programmes were in the same building, but nevertheless there was a boundary between the two groups that constructed different identities not only for the children, but also for the teachers. These identities were interrelated in the sense that the teachers positioned children differently when they crossed the boundary and, in turn, positioned themselves differently, either as teachers of the babies or of the toddlers. Indeed, teachers of the under-twos referred to the teachers of the toddlers as 'those out there'.

Background to the Aotearoa/New Zealand context

Within New Zealand there are a range of diverse early childhood education and care settings. The two most common are centres that offer mixed-age settings and those that offer separate peer groupings. This latter option has developed as a result of New Zealand's history and the influence of childcare regulations (May 2003). In 1960, in response to a scandal around baby farming, the New Zealand government brought childcare centres under the responsibility of the Child Welfare Division of the Department of Education (1960). This was the first distinct nationally mandated separation between care and education. These regulations also made a distinction in the needs of children based on their ages. Children under 2 years old were identified as needing lower ratios, less space for play, and different health and safety standards (Nicholson 2002). This split into under-two- and over-two-year-old services is still reflected in current legislation (New Zealand Government 1998). It is particularly evident in funding and licensing requirements. The defining of under-two- and over-two-year-old children can therefore be seen as a historical and legislative construction, which is still being endorsed by current legislation.

These funding structures and their associated philosophical beliefs encouraged a number of centres to develop at least two separate areas, usually under- and over-two, although some centres also have a toddler area. Centres that operate toddler areas separately from 'preschool' do so for philosophical reasons, rather than funding, as toddlers and preschoolers are both funded at the over-two rates.

All early childhood education and care centres are required by the early childhood regulations to develop a transition to school policy. Most centres that operate peer groupings also extend this practice by developing a transition policy to support children through the process of transition from one area to another within the centre.

My philosophical position on transition within early childhood centres has been challenged recently in both my role as a lecturer in an undergraduate early childhood teaching degree programme at the University of Waikato and as National President of Te Tari Puna Ora O Aotearoa New Zealand Childcare Association (NZCA), an association which has had considerable influence on government policy, legislation and initiatives in the early childhood sector during the past 40 years. NZCA has recently had significant involvement in a number of government early childhood initiatives, including the development of Pathways to the Future: Nga Huarahi Arataki (Ministry of Education 2002), a review of the Early Childhood Regulations and a review of funding of the early childhood sector. Involvement in these initiatives generated a lot of discussion in the early childhood sector, and challenged the current policies and philosophies held by a number of teachers, and early childhood service operators including myself. Some of these discussions and debates, in particular those that focused on group size and funding rates based on age difference, for example, under- and over-twos kindled my interest in transition from one group to another within one centre. During some of these discussions I began to be interested in the idea of different social worlds and boundaries.

The case study

The theoretical underpinning for this research is based on symbolic interaction theory and explores the notion of the under-twos, the toddlers and the preschoolers as being three different social worlds where the children move from one social world to another. I wanted to explore whether there were any associated shifts in relationships, expectations and identities in the transition from under-twos to toddlers.

The case study centre

The centre that provided data for this research is operated by a well-established Community Trust, and is licensed for 34 over-twos and 12 under-twos. The under-two area has a staffing ratio of one to four including a long-standing supervisor, whilst the over-two ratio is one to six with both a supervisor and an assistant supervisor. The under-twos, toddlers and preschoolers are housed in a large building with three distinctly separate areas for the three age groups. All three programmes also have their own separate outside areas. Due to staff ratios, the toddler area children and staff combine with the preschool area early in the morning and at the end of the day. Sometimes, the toddlers also return to the under-two area, until all the staff are present. The toddlers also combine with the preschool children for lunch and sleep time then return to their area in the afternoon.

During the time that this research was being undertaken there were considerable staff changes taking place throughout the centre. Staff were taking parental leave, moving to another city and moving on to other positions within the early childhood sector. These changes may have had some influence on the research outcomes. They are, however, balanced by long-standing staff members who have worked for the Trust for many years.

The transition programme in this centre is based on a comprehensive transition policy, which was under review at the time of this research. Time constraints appear to have influenced the implementation of the process. This is a busy centre, with staff allocated to three different areas and it is not possible for all of the staff to spend time planning for transitions. Paid, 2-hour staff meetings are held once a fortnight. These meetings take place at the end of the day, outside operating hours. The agenda for these meetings includes curriculum planning, housekeeping, any particular issues that have arisen since the last meeting, some professional development and discussions about transition. Although many centres in New Zealand do not have staff meetings outside operating hours, there was a general feeling from these staff that there was still not enough time available to dedicate solely to transition planning. One of the teachers commented that there is 'just lack of time for support teachers to get together to plan transition, to develop transition plans really'.

As noted earlier, these divisions by age are as much determined by funding requirements as by a consideration of educational requirements. However, they may, at the same time, construct new social and educational worlds and new identities.

Identity

Constructing identities

Damhorst (2001) has elaborated on symbolic interaction theory with a focus on the construction of self and identity. Damhorst presents symbolic inter-action theory as being based on a broad set of premises about how an in-dividual's self is defined. The first premise is that the self is defined through interactions with others. It is contended that one's sense of oneself can only be developed through interactions with other people:

> Other people respond to an individual (both verbally and non-verbally) about how he or she is doing, what he or she is supposed to be doing, what the value or worth of that individual is, and how the individual is identified. Other people's responses shape how an in-dividual defines the self. (Damhorst 2001:1)

Symbolic interaction theory is presented as being an active theory of self-development. Unlike some theories that propose an individual should be passive to the rules imposed by society, symbolic interaction theory views an individual to be active in the process. This is demonstrated through the belief that individuals act on the environment to test out behaviours. Based on feedback, an individual makes active choices, then decides to accept or reject other views.

Damhorst identified three categories of people from whom we seek feedback. First, significant others—people whose opinions have an important impact on the self, such as parents and best friends. Secondly, reference groups—groups to whom the individual looks for ideas on how to think and behave. Thirdly, generalized others—the general notion of what people on the whole think of us.

The concept of self has been conceptualized by theorists as a *'social pro-duct'* that emerges through relationships with others. How a person perceives the way others view them, influences their self-concept, thus selves are so-cially influenced through interactions with others: 'Selves are created within contexts and take into account the values, norms and mores of the others likely to participate in that context' (Oyserman 2004:12).

Oyserman (2004) suggests that identity is contextual and that each in-dividual's identity is given meaning in the context of the individual's re-lationship to others and the individual's place within the social group, and therefore in her view the self is a cognitive construction, which is developed through social interactions and experience drawn from membership of groups.

Self has a number of dimensions, which include, representations from the past (personal history), the future (possible selves) and the present. Individual's personal histories play an important role in their identities. Their histories assess their abilities, personalities and self-worth, which are embedded within these memories from the past. Their memories help to shape an individual's view of themselves, for example, 'I am a good dancer'; 'I'm not a good driver'. Personal histories also contribute to a sense of well-being and influence current behaviour. Happy memories tend to contribute to positive behaviour, whereas unhappy memories influence negative behaviour.

There are some variations across disciplines and methodologies as to the meaning of 'self-concept'. Oyserman describes self-concept as a set of ideas about who we are. She maintains that the self is an active agent, which plays a part in seeking competence, resolutions of conflict and mastery, which is influenced and shaped by early experiences and relationships. A dimension of the self that is connected with self-concept is self-esteem or a sense of well-being. Oyserman (2004) describes how individuals whose self-concepts include good self-esteem appear to be more motivated and resilient and who are able to cope much better than individuals who have negative views of their identity.

Identity as a confident, competent learner in transitions

Children experience a shift in their perception of themselves when they feel they have become 'a competent Kindergarten child' and go through a role reorganization when they go into a new situation (Griebel and Niesel 1997). Griebel and Niesel maintained that when children begin school they have to learn the social rules that are acceptable to that community. These rules may include some set rules for that particular setting, for example, 'you have to line up when the bell rings', 'you have to put your hand up to talk with the teacher'. Other rules encompass more generalized expectations of social behaviour. Children are expected to be considerate to one another, to respect the school environment and so on (Juvonen and Wentzel, 1996). When children embrace the social norms of their school context, they are able to act in a social manner, which will be approved by their teachers and peers. Jovonen and Wentzel (1996) found that social approval results in a heightened feeling of belonging, a sense of connection with others that, in turn, promotes children's participation in school activities and strengthens their identification with the school culture.

Teachers can play a vital role in the child's developing sense of identity in the context of an educational setting (Pollard and Filer 1996). Pollard and Filer maintain that how teachers interact with children can influence the way the children see themselves, thus impacting on their own identity. Their research indicates that teachers can be perceived as 'significant others' in the child's life.

Children develop a sense of themselves as competent learners and capable people (Ministry of Education 1996:9) when they are able to work through the daily challenges in the early childhood environment, including both social and curriculum challenges. Feeling competent and capable is important for children's continued learning, development and sense of self. Feeling competent in everyday activities in a number of settings should be a factor to take into consideration during any transition process. McNaughton (1998) believes that children can engage effectively in classroom activities when there is a similarity between the expertise situated in everyday early childhood settings and the expertise situated in school. McNaughton maintains this involves sharing understandings and pedagogical approaches across the two settings, and teachers valuing the educational experiences offered in each setting and taking steps to ensure that there is some continuity in the activities offered between the settings.

Much of the literature on transition indicates that children who have been supported to explore and develop a strong sense of themselves are less likely to experience stress in the transition from one environment to another. This sense of identity seems central in a child's ability to persevere in a new and potentially stressful situation. Knowing who you are, your strengths and limitations, and having developed relationships that include trust and reliance during those times of insecurity seems to increase the likelihood of a positive experience.

The findings

Expert to novice

The notion of developing a sense of one's self is featured in the literature on symbolic interaction theory. In this study, there is evidence that, as children move from the social world of 'under-twos' to the social world of 'toddlers', they are experiencing social construction in their attempts to learn the new social rules, understand the social cues and try to gain an insight into how new adults perceive them in this new world or environment. As children reach the end of their time in the under-two area, they are often the 'expert' within their peer group. They have developed a strong sense of themselves in this social world as competent learners in familiar surroundings. However, when they begin the transition into the world of the 'toddlers', they are the youngest in this group and are a novice in this new environment. They have to learn how to act as a toddler, gain an understanding of the expectations of their new peers and the adults, and cope with the challenges of being a 'novice' in their new surroundings.

This transition from being in an environment where the child is confident and competent in the routines, rules and expectations, where he or she can show leadership with younger children to a new environment where everything is new, is featured in the literature on transition to school. Some of the transition to school literature suggests that optimum discontinuities are a positive feature for education—'teachable moments may also emerge in the context of certain critical events, usually times when children are vulnerable or challenged, and thus more open to environmental influences' (Bailey 2002:291). For some children, however, the discontinuities may not be positive because there are too many. One teacher gave an example of this from a transition that was taking place in the toddler area during this research project. The implicit viewpoint here from the interviewee was that it is an inevitable part of growing up to be seen as the leader and grown-up in one place, and then to be 'at the bottom of the heap' in the next place.

> We have a child at the moment who has come from the baby room and was very much kingpin [in the under-twos] and often it is sort of demonstrated in their behaviour, and sometimes not very sociable behaviour. And it is almost like they've been brought down a peg or two ... when they have been put with the older ones. (Chris, teacher preschool/toddlers)

One parent said that she felt it must be strange when you have been the oldest in your peer group for some time, and then suddenly you turn two and move to a different place with different children. She felt that maintaining a sense of self could be stressful for a young child, especially if you are the oldest in your group, and suddenly you are with a number of other children your own age and older. 'Whereas he was the only eighteen-month or two-year old in the babies [under-twos], suddenly there is twelve of them' (Sally, parent toddlers).

Children, teachers and parents navigating their way through the rules and different expectations

Learning the social rules and having to act in certain situations becomes clearer when the toddlers join with the preschool group during different periods of the day. Sally, a parent in the toddler area, said that her son was able to fit with expectations of the preschool staff very quickly once he understood the rules. She described how understanding the rules helped him to negotiate his way around the environment smoothly:

> The rules, and how it works, like I mean, Pat [teacher] says he comes out and says 'can I come to mat time today' and Pat says, 'Only if you sit quietly'. And he sits down and crosses his legs, and follows all the kids. He knows what he has to do to be a 'preschooler'. (Sally, parent toddlers)

Children's understanding of the rules and the teachers' expectations of the younger children moving from the under-two area can cause some frustrations for both the children and the teachers. One staff member indicated that at times the staff members' expectations might be unrealistic of the capabilities of the young age group. Chris (teacher, preschool/toddlers) said that, in her view, under-twos and toddlers are different. She indicated that staff in the under-two area view the children differently from the staff in the toddler area and therefore their expectations are different. Staff members within the toddler's area appeared to have higher expectations. It was almost as if once children turn 2 years of age the toddler staff expect them to take more responsibility for their own actions, begin to understand consequences and become more independent of adult support:

> I think that ... the major idea around expectations ... comes with the ages, that staff expect, well staff who normally work with children who are three or four expect more from toddlers—expect them to know where things are and expect them not to eat the lids off the pens. [Laughter]. Little things like that. And you know, like I said before, it's just a case of being able to monitor that but that's difficult and so you can feel quite cross that all your pens have been eaten again, or that the wall has been drawn on and not the paper [laughter]. So that there are expectations that children will follow social rules but they don't—and people understand that they don't, but it still doesn't stop the expectation that they should at some point. (Chris, teacher preschool/toddlers)

The toddler area appears to have more of a focus on exploration and independence and so has a shift in the emphasis and expectations from that of the under-twos. It was also apparent during interviews with toddler staff and parents that there were different philosophies and expectation being implemented within each area:

> I think generally there is an underpinning philosophy to the whole centre, but also yes, people do have personal philosophies and interpretation of philosophies, and I think it is different for each room because there are very different people in it. (Chris, teacher preschool/toddlers)

One staff member noted that the differences in the philosophies were evident through the expectations of the staff members in the toddler area. For example, there is much more emphasis on the toddlers taking responsibility for their own belongings during the day-to-day routines of the centre:

Expectations are linked to philosophy, so yeh I would say that they are quite different because, especially like in terms of personal belongings and knowing where their own things are and getting them all the time, [shoes and hats] before they can go outside, they are different. (Emma, teacher under-twos)

This difference in philosophy and practice is also reflected in the expectations of children. The toddler area supports children in their growing sense of self and the development of their own identity. This is evident in Lisa's (parent) comments about development of self-awareness, and how this is reflected in areas such as social activities and fashion. She suggested that toddlers are in limbo between the cultures of under-twos and preschool:

Especially the preschool group, they are suddenly interested in what they are wearing and who's been to what, and who has their party at where, and who eats what food, and what they're allowed to do and what they're not, and what the rules are for things. Whereas under-twos specifically, don't really care what they're wearing, they either eat or they don't eat, if they like something they like, if they don't like it they don't like it, but they're probably interested if someone else has cake, but they're probably not too worried about who has ham sandwiches. They are much more egocentric in a sense I suppose. Whereas when they're preschool they seem to be far more 'group' conscious, and even to the point where if someone's going to kindy—kindy is the thing to do because so-and-so is going to kindy. And I guess, the middle group [toddlers] is just trying to find it's way really and starting to become aware of those things. And I guess the transition from that little group, is the transition group for life skills. (Lisa, parent toddlers)

A shift in curriculum from well-being to exploration and to contribution

There was a perceived contrast between the toddlers and the under-two philosophy which has an emphasis on nurturing and well-being:

I think that probably in the babies there is that more kind of nurturing and well-being type thing kind of going on, and I guess in the toddlers and preschool, for me, would be for me, especially in the toddlers it would probably be more of an exploration type thing going on really. There's a huge focus for that age group—getting in and stuck in to everything ... and as they get older—the same thing, it is a lot of exploration but a lot more contribution for the preschool age children. (Sally, parent toddlers)

The five strands of the national curriculum (Ministry of Education 1996) are well-being, belonging, communication, exploration and contribution. Sally, a parent of a toddler, is suggesting that these have a sequence with age. Once a transition to the toddler area has occurred children are expected to do more for themselves and take on a greater level of independence, as highlighted by Emma:

> Probably the biggest one that's struck me is in terms of personal belongings because like the toddlers that are just going out there, you hear them being asked to go and find their shoes and put their shoes on, or find their own hats, but sometimes they will help get them but that's quite a big jump, from a day before you're two 'til you're two, kind of thing ... Even something like washing their hands, because we don't have a hand basin in here, so now they've got to go and wash their hands and dry them, and do it well but not flood the bathroom [laughter]. (Emma, teacher under-twos)

A parent commented on the shift in expectations on children when they move out of the under-two area:

> I mean it's like how people talk about children going to school, they are in childcare or whatever, well you say they are four type thing, and as soon as they turn five, there are different expectations. I think there is too, especially the ones coming out of the baby room, a lot of them still are only babies—they are only just two—whereas they are kind of hurled into here and the expectations are a lot higher I think. (Sally, parent toddlers)

A teacher also commented on this in terms of focus and expectations being different with different children. She likens this to ages and stages of development. She said,

> I think if you were going to sum that up—I would say that it was strong throughout the Centre [different expectations] ... and that there are different focuses as they change, so that the focus with very, very young children may be more on their physical development and on their language development, and then as they come through it tends be social development and in to their intellectual development. (Chris, teacher preschool/toddlers)

Once again, this time using a different framework from the national curriculum, a sequence by age is suggested (physical, language, social and intellectual). The notion of holistic or integrated curriculum gives way in attempts to make sense of transition.

Lisa, a parent in the toddler area, took the view that different expectations based on age levels is a positive aspect of transition for children moving into different areas within the centre. She commented, 'I think if you do separate out the ages there is much more chance you can focus on their developmental needs, yes, and I have certainly seen evidence of that here' (Lisa, parent toddlers).

Lisa went on to discuss how she felt her daughter was ready to move on to work in a more formal way when she was ready to move into the preschool section in the previous childcare centre that they had attended. She commented, 'She was ready to do stuff, writing and stuff like that' (Lisa, parent toddlers).

Implications for practice

This was a case study of a transition programme from under-twos to a toddler programme in one childcare centre at one point in time. Although it by no means describes all the transition practices of that childcare centre at the time, and certainly not even 6 months later, the perceptions of four teachers and two parents raised interesting issues about transition within a centre. The separation of under-twos and over-twos has been, at least in part, a consequence of funding and legislation. As a result, it appears that teachers and families were finding differences between under-two-year-olds and toddlers, in order to provide a developmental rationale for the separation and to make sense of the constructed boundaries and identities.

Over-twos were described as 'busy', 'independent' and not in need of 'hugs' in the same way as under-twos. The curriculum was described as being appropriately different for each age group: a focus on well-being, language and physical development for under-twos; a focus on exploration, contribution, social and intellectual development for the over-twos. Current views of integrated curriculum do not support such constructions of age specific curriculum and, in fact, the under-twos curriculum included mathematics and 'letters', and teachers were concerned about the well-being and belonging of the over-twos.

It seems likely that these expected differences were constructing expectations and identities for the children. In any event, they created discontinuities both for parents and children. The interviewees saw these discontinuities as, on the whole, negative, but mostly inevitable. The view was expressed that it was inevitable for children to become 'kingpins' in one social world and then be 'novices' in the next, and that this is just part of life. Transition was, in a sense, seen as a stumbling block, not as a learning opportunity, and assessment did not cover the actual transition process. I have argued that the transition, in part, should be documented through assessments. It is certainly true that early childhood education and care is a time for children to learn to cope with change and challenge. It is also my view that challenges constructed by the adults, associated with transition, need to be carefully managed and supported. The process will have a different impact on different children, and this research has highlighted the potential influence of transition on children's sense of identity as competent learners.

This research project draws on a small sample of participants. It is a case study of one childcare centre at one particular point in time and cannot be generalized to all early childhood transitions or even to this centre 6 months later. What this study can do is 'generalize to a theory' (Firestone 1993). In this case, it is that educational institutions can construct expectations, social worlds and identities by the way they group children. This construction of age-group expectations is not, of itself, a good or a bad thing, but it is a construction, not a developmental inevitability, and teachers need to be reflective about it by comparing this interpretation with their own situation.

References

Bailey, D.B. (2002) Are critical periods critical for early childhood education? The role of timing in early childhood pedagogy, *Early Childhood Research Quarterly*, 17: 281–94.

Damhorst, M.I. (2001) Symbolic Interaction Theory. Available at: http://www.fca.iastate.edu/classweb/fall2002/TC467/assignments/SltheoryX (accessed 15 August 2003).

Department of Education (1960) *New Zealand Early Childhood Regulations*. Wellington: Government Print.

Firestone, W.A. (1993) Alternative arguments for generalizing from data as applied to qualitative research, *Educational Researcher*, 22(4): 16–23.

Griebel, W. & Niesel, R. (1997) From family to kindergarten: A common experience in a transition perspective. Paper presented at 7th Conference on the Quality of Early Childhood Education 'Children in a Changing Society', *European Early Childhood Education Research Association*, Munich, Germany, 3–6 September 1997.

Juvonen, J. and Wentzel, K. (eds) (1996) *Social Motivation. Understanding Children's School Adjustment*. Cambridge: Press Syndicate.

McNaughton, S. (1998) Activating developmental process over the transition to school. *Childrens Issues Journal* 2(1): 34–8.

Ministry of Education (1996) *Te Whariki He Whariki Matauranga Mo Nga Mokopuna o Aotearoa Early Childhood Curriculum*. Wellington: Learning Media.

Ministry of Education (2002) *Pathways to the Future: Nga Huarahi Arataki.* Wellington: Learning Media

New Zealand Government (1998) *Education (Early Childhood Centres) Regulations.* Wellington: Government Print.

Nicholson, C. (2002) *Transition.* Unpublished paper, School of Education, University of Waikato, Hamilton.

Oyserman, D. (2004) Self-concept and identity, in M. B. Brewer and M. Hewstone (eds) *Self and Social Identity.* Oxford: Blackwell Publishing.

Pollard, A. with Filer, A. (1996) *The Social World of Children's Learning. Case Studies of Pupils from Four to Seven.* London: Cassell.

CHILDREN EXPERIENCING TRANSITION

By the time children enter statutory education they may have already attended a number of educational settings. Each of these experiences is likely to affect them and their capacity to learn. Such is the significance of early transitions for young children that it is essential that parents, educators and policy makers pay close attention to their experiences in order to provide well for them. How the transition is for the children themselves as they move from one phase of education to another is addressed in this section.

The first chapter explores the need to develop links that facilitate the transition to school by influencing the development of children's motivation to learn. Broström calls learning about the different ways of learning in a new setting a 'transitory activity system' as it serves as a vehicle for transmitting information about the learning styles in the next phase of education. He suggests that to avoid the culture shock at transition it is not sufficient to build an understanding of the physical differences, but there is also a need to build a transition in children's thinking.

Legislation on children's rights demands that children have a chance to express their own views and have influence on their lives. This, and the view of children as having knowledge and being experts on their own lives, has brought about a growing interest in taking account of children's perspectives on matters concerning them. Children's competence to participate in research and express their views has also been acknowledged, and research with children has shown that children are reliable sources who give valuable information if the right methods are used. This section therefore asks: How do children experience the transition to school? What are their concerns, expectations, and anticipations? What do different studies reveal and are there commonalities among these studies?

The final chapter in this section considers what happens over the course of a school day such as arrival and departure procedures, playground interactions and learning the school culture. The focus is on the changing demands on children, particularly relating to the independence they are expected to demonstrate in school settings in terms of knowledge and skills, understanding the rules, adjusting to the physical context of the school and accepting the educational environment of the school.

5 Transitions in children's thinking

Stig Broström

Research shows that too many children experience the transition to school as a culture shock. For this reason, over the last decade, teachers have implemented so-called transition activities, such as mutual visits before school starts, in order to make a bridge to school. One might name this an 'organizational transition system'. However, transition to school also calls for the development of higher mental functions, often identified as development of meta-cognition or learning motive. Seen from the perspective of activity theory, transition to formal education entails crossing boundaries from the activity system of play to the activity system of school learning, so leading to the development of learning motive. To facilitate children's transition to school preschool teachers should provide activities which influence the development of children's motivation to learn. One might name such transition activities 'educational transition activities', in other words, creating a 'transitory activity system'. Using different types of advanced play (for example frame play, aesthetic play and play-drama) one might build such a 'transitory activity system', which mediates between the two systems (play and school learning), and with that contribute to the development of children's motivation to learn.

The chapter entails theoretical reflection on a transitory activity system and ends up with a very rough framework defined as a row of connected activities: reading of good literature—literature dialogues—drawing and painting—frame play—and dialogues with children on their play constructions.

Introduction: transition

In many countries the period of early childhood is fragmented and split up in different arenas of responsibility. Children may spend only a few years in the different areas before they transit to another arena. For example, in Denmark most children transit from infant care to preschool, and again to kindergarten class and leisure-time centre in a period of 1–6 years.

Because children have experiences with transition from their early years, one might suggest that they have accumulated transition competencies, making them transition experts who are able to move successfully through the transition from preschool to school. However, international research on starting school suggests that moving from preschool to school can be challenging, if not traumatic, for some children and especially for children with less-than-optimal circumstances (for example, Broström 2002a; Shore 1998; Wagner 2003).

International transition literature describes a number of problems to overcome as we strive to help children make a successful transition to school (for example, Broström and Wagner 2003; Fabian and Dunlop 2002). For example, there are big educational differences between preschool and school (Broström 1999a, 2001); there is a lack of communication between kindergarten and school; some children have a hazy and outdated picture of school, and some Nordic research shows that a number of children expect school to be an authoritarian place (Broström 2003a; Lillemyr 2001).

It is in this context that in recent years and across the world parents, preschools and schools have cooperated with each other in order to make up transition activities. Reports and research from practice describe various approaches and types of transition activities, but in general a double approach seems to be stressed, namely 'a school ready preschool' and 'a child ready school'. A *school-ready-preschool* is one that focuses on developing curricula and educational practice, which on the one hand focuses on children's interest and own value and, on the other hand, also includes content and form that help children to become school ready. A *child-ready-school* has meetings with the preschool teachers in order to learn about the individual child and the relations between the children, which helps the teachers to create a fruitful relationship with each child and to challenge the child appropriately.

In general, transition theory and practice strive to combine the most important arenas in the child's life during the transition process to school, to help children to experience continuity and to see life as a unified whole with a clear progression. Thus, transition activities are usually expressed in terms of cooperation between parents, preschool and schools. Examples of activities included in transition programmes in a Danish investigation (Broström 2002a) described 32 different activities, such as the parents and the child, and also preschool teachers and the group of children, visiting the school and the kindergarten class before school starts, and the preschool teachers and school teachers having conferences before school starts about children's life and development. These activities reflect cooperation.

Effectiveness in transition

When teachers plan such a large number of transition activities, they have a logical hope that the children involved will experience a successful transition. Oddly enough, some children who have had lots of transition experiences do not manage the transition very well and they do not feel suitable in school. Thus, many preschool teachers and school teachers report that a number of well functioning preschool children actually seem to lose some competencies in the transition to school. A case study (Broström 2003b) focused on this illogical phenomenon. Preschool teachers described some children about to start school as independent, actively inquisitive and exploring persons, who also functioned well with peers. However, the case study showed that during the first weeks in school these children changed attitudes and became less active, expressing a form of insecurity. Although most of these children had obtained the necessary level of school readiness, they did not feel good in school, which impacted on their well being and was a hindrance to their being active learners in the new environment. Another concern is that this (temporary) loss of competence might pave the way for poor self-esteem and insecurity in the new setting.

Here a paradox is expressed. How can active and independent children be transformed into people dominated by reserve and insecurity? How can this be understood? Elsewhere (Broström, 2003b), I have argued that the paradox can be understood in the light of a theoretical framework of situated learning (Cole et al. 1971; Rogoff 1990; Lave and Wenger 1991; Lave 1997). A Vygotskian view argues for the idea that the child's *individual* learning comes into existence in a whole, which consists of interactions between the child and the surrounding objects and people. Lave and Wenger (1991) argue for *social* and *contextual* learning, which happens in, and is bound by, a specific shared, social practice. Thus, learning is embedded in, and tied to, a specific situation. Learning is situated. Such a systemic and contextual view does not regard the child's learning as a cognitive structure existing solely within the child, but rather as accessing shared social knowledge and skills, learned in and related to a shared social practice. Thus, the idea of situated learning could be a leading hypothesis in order to understand the fact that some children seem to risk losing existing competencies as they start school. From my point of view, this calls for a transition approach supporting the development of the child's individual thinking, so allowing the child to act in a much more independent and context free way. Thus, I would like to see preschool programmes focus on developing thinking skills that are not contextually bound. Still recognizing the importance of learning as a social process, children could be helped to look at ways they could use common thinking skills in different contexts. Maybe a Vygotskian approach can be taken into account in the development of a new transition model and practice.

From external transition activities to interior transition system

The studies mentioned above seem to show that it is not enough to make use of practical organizational transition activities, such as mutual visits and information, which help the child to become more familiar with the setting he/she will transit to in the future. Although it is of importance to extend the range and intensity of such external and organizational transition activities, we also need to reflect more on developing the child's thinking and conscious reflection. If the child has more knowledge about why, how and what he/she has learnt in preschool, this might help him/her to act more independently and consciously in the new environment. This refers to the scope of the children's self-awareness and understanding of their learning, or according to Leont'ev (1978, 1981) the scope of their motivation to learn (learning motive).

However, not any activity will contribute to this aspect of the child's development. Referring to Vygotsky (1978), particular activities in the zone of proximal development will start new processes of development. That means activities that challenge the child and contain demands, which he or she is not yet able to handle alone. Under adult guidance or in collaboration with more capable peers, the child can raise his or her actions to a more advanced level. Often this kind of activity has a powerful impact on the development of the individual. It is a turning point, a revelation referred to as 'learning by expanding' (Engeström 1987).

From a cultural-historical understanding, *play* seems to be a form of activity that reflects the above mentioned qualities (Elkonin 1980). Through play, new knowledge, skills and actions often appear so it can be assumed that play can serve as transition tool in order to create a more complex thinking. In this way, play is seen as a transitory activity, an activity which leads the development of higher mental functions (see an analysis of play in Broström 1999b).

Play as transitory activity

However, the optimistic idea that play automatically has a leading and developmental function, such as regarding play as a pivot for the automatic development of the child's psyche (Leont'ev 1978), has been over interpreted. In a similar way, the Vygotskian phrase 'in play a child always behaves beyond his average age' has been misunderstood to mean that play always leads to a more advanced level of development: such an understanding has been discussed and criticized. For example, van der Veer and Valsiner (1991) argue that play does not in itself contribute to the child's development. From their point of view, play only has a developmental potential when the play environment holds a possibility to challenge children to cross their zone of proximal development. In continuation of this argument, Wood and Attifeld (1996) define such an environment as a place that promotes interaction between playmates, and builds relationships between children and teachers.

In these environments, the teacher plays an active role, far beyond that of only observing with a wait-and-see attitude (Vygotsky 1993). Vygotsky can be interpreted as arguing for a challenging and supporting function in play, aimed to develop children's zone of proximal development (Vygotsky 1978; Newman and Holzman 1993). However, this is not a process that happens automatically. Learning and development through play demands what Holzman (1997) calls *interaction of creative imitations and implementation*. That means play sequences that not only reproduce the surrounding world, but create new dimensions.

When creative imitations and implementation characterize play, new moments of learning can appear. This gives the possibility to go beyond the current contextual frame. Children not only play in agreement with the common theme, they also expand beyond it as well. Such play activities are characterized by changes and the appearance of new contents. According to Engeström (1987), through such activities new knowledge, skills and actions often will appear. For that reason Engeström names this kind of learning activity 'learning by expanding'. In some kinds of play we see such episodes, but while young children's leading activity is play, as opposed to learning, this type of activity can be named expansive play (Broström 1999b). However, such expanding elements do not appear automatically. Children have to be provided with suitable raw material. In some recent research (Broström 2005), an environment with such elements was provided when the teachers combined play with reading of literature of high quality and literature dialogues and also a goal-directed use of tools and signs (Vygotsky 1978).

Using different kinds of 'expansive play' (frame-play, aesthetical play, drama-play), the boundaries of 'free' play will be crossed. Such kinds of play can be seen as an activity situated between two activity systems: play and school learning. Thus, this can be described as a transitory activity that has the potential to enrich the individual child and to guide the development of motivation. However, at the same time it could also be seen as an activity that will bridge preschool and school.

Seen from the perspective of activity theory (Leont'ev 1981), transition to formal education entails crossing boundaries from the activity system of play to the activity system of school learning. The two activity systems are developed in response to different needs, and entail different rules, tools and divisions of labour (Baumer 2003). The transition can be facilitated by developing a transitory activity system that mediates between these two systems, ensuring that the result of one activity system serves as tool in the next activity system (Baumer et al. in press).

Play as transitory activity system contributes to the development of children's learning motive (Leont'ev 1981) by using of children's storytelling (Broström 2002b), the concept of frame-play (Broström, 1996, 1997, 1999a,b), aesthetic theme play (Lindqvist 1995), and play-drama (Baumer et al. in press).

Frame play

Through year-long experiences with role play in general 6-year-olds are conscious of the imaginary play situation (Elkonin 1980), that is, the concrete situation they imagine. The development of this new level of play makes it possible to introduce frame play (Broström 1996, 1997, 1999b), in which children and the teacher plan and play together. On the basis of common experiences, for example, a field trip or a story the children themselves have created, they decide a general theme, such as 'What happens in the witch's forest?' or a theme with more social realism. The theme functions as a shared frame that the children use steadily and for a long time. However, to enable them to carry through a complex, shared frame play, the children need a shared imagination and development of the theme (Garvey 1976: 578–579), that is, they need to create a common understanding of the imaginary play situation.

Teachers and children plan the play and decide the content, or to use Bateson's (1972) words—the text—and with that they give some signals how to interpret the message or the content, which helps the play participants to understand each other. According to Bateson (1972), the establishment of the context is a psychological frame. The function of a psychological frame is to include certain messages and actions, and to exclude others. A psychological frame has the same function as a picture frame: it tells the spectator what he or she should notice, namely, what is within the frame. Thus, the frame defines the premises.

In frame play the children's consciousness of the psychological frame is strengthened through the establishment of a real, existing frame. Children construct the frame for example when they turn the classroom into a hospital with a casualty and operating theatre. Supported by this physical frame, children and preschool teachers imagine themes, roles and actions. In other words: 'they share a fantasy, which they collectively construct and modify' (Fine 1983: 12), and like this they develop a *collective fantasy*.

Because it is necessary for 6-year-olds to support their imagination, the teachers ask the children to express their decisions verbally, and also in creative drawings and paintings, which serve as models. As pointed out by

Davydov (1977), Aidarova (1982) and Venger (1985), such models help to develop a new self-esteem and consciousness of children's own activity, as well as incipient reflective thought.

In frame play, several elements are decided on beforehand among the children and the adults. Because there is a certain time interval between the formulation of the plan and realization of the play, the roles, rules and actions are prepared thoroughly. There are also accessories to organize for the play, such as aprons and money for going shopping in the store and restaurant. In this way, the frame play is more organized and more purposeful than role play. The play motive in frame play is different from the motive in role play. In role play the motive lies in the play itself. In frame play the motive is shifting more and more toward the result of the play activity.

Tools and symbols in frame play

When children build up the physical setting of the play and fill up the setting with equipment and accessories for the play—such as an emergency telephone, the hose, car phones, helmets for the firemen—these objects or tools have an influence on the play. In such a frame, children produce different forms of texts. In one study, the children involved in frame play also produced different forms of text to support and develop their play frame. With help from their teacher, they wrote several noticeboards of information to identify the functions of their constructed setting, for example, restaurant, bus station, kiosk (Broström 2003b).

According to Vygotsky (1978), signs and tools have a mediating function. Although signs and tools diverge, the basic analogy between them rests on the mediating function. In this way, Vygotsky (1978: 54) shows that both signs and tools can be subsumed under the more general concept of indirect (mediated) activity.

However, signs and tools have different functions:

> The tool's function is to serve as the conductor of human influence on the object of activity; it is *externally* oriented; it must lead to changes in objects. It is a means by which human external activity is aimed at mastering, and triumphing over, nature. The sign on the other hand, changes nothing in the object of psychological operation. It is a means of internal activity aimed at mastering oneself; the sign is *internally* oriented. (Vygotsky 1978: 55)

According to Vygotsky (1978: 55) the use of tools and signs will contribute to more advanced activities and psychological operations: '. . . the use of tools limitlessly broadens the range of activities within which the new psychological functions may operate. In this context, we can use the term *higher* psychological function, or *higher behavioral* as referring to the combination of tool and sign in psychological activity' (Vygotsky 1978: 55).

Signs

Vygotsky (1985,) assumes that signs, including speech, writing, number, drawing, symbols, manage and mediate higher mental functions (such as attention and perception). In a view that contrasts with that of Vygotsky, Piaget (1964) distinguishes between signs and symbols. According to Piaget (1964), there exists a likeness between the symbol (signifiant), and the thing or person that the symbol stands for (signifié). For example, the symbol of an anchor relates in a visible way to the maritime. The opposing view to this is that the sign is defined as an arbitrary indicator (signifiant), and there is no resemblance between what the sign stands for and what it indicates. According to this view, the signs are artificial, because they do look like what they refer to at all. For example, the following constellation of letters that make up the word HOUSE do not look like a house.

In children's own play they use symbols. Play is carried out by means of symbols. In one child's play a boy pretended to be a fireman and at the same time he ascribed a subjective meaning to the chair: the chair as a fire engine. To be able to play the child has to concentrate on the idea of the activity: the chair is not a chair, but the front seat of the fire engine; I am not Peter, but a fireman. In Bateson's (1972) terms, the child masters the paradox: I am not a fireman I pretend I am a fireman. From this it could be assumed that role play or symbolic play influences the child's mind.

However, because signs (such as the word house) in relation to symbols (such as the child's drawing of a house) have a higher level of abstraction, maybe children's use of signs will have a more direct impact on the development of higher mental functions, and moreover could serve as a means for developing of reading and writing skills.

In an example of frame play, 'life in the forest' (Broström 1999b), inspired by a visit to a forest supervisor, some 6-year-old children built up the forest supervisor's office. Two girls planned to be clerks working in the office. They arranged the desk with a telephone so that they could receive and place an order. When some children phoned for a truck load of firewood, the girls eagerly passed on the order to some boys playing truck drivers. An observing teacher provided the girls with order books, order forms and writing materials. Immediately, the girls engaged with the tools, which led to reading and writing activities.

If the teacher is able to offer the children relevant literacy materials, which are in agreement with the premises of the play, the children will engage themselves in meaningful reading and writing activities. Christie (1994) illustrates different types of literacy materials (functional literacy props), which might be useful in children's role play. For instance, in restaurant play it might be useful to provide the setting with the following functional literacy props: pencils, pens, markers, note pads, bank checks, wall signs (supermarket), shelf labels for store areas (meat), and product containers (Christie 1994). Using such form of signs in play in this way may well involve children using higher mental functions.

Tools

Tools have another kind of mediating function. Tools—and, in general, the objects—that the child uses in play, affect the play activity and the object of the play. The tool, the object or the cultural artefact, is 'a material object, which is modified of mankind and used as means to regulate their interaction with the surrounding world and each other' (Cole 1990: 7).

In play children's use of tools have this regulating function. For instance, in a fireman play the actions were mediated by means of the following artefacts: the telephone, the walkie-talkie, the control desk, the fire engine, the hose and other equipment. Because the boys involved in the play had built up an office at the fire station with phones and a control desk, and also constructed a fire engine, these artefacts mediated the play activity. For instance, a boy pretended to be a fireman calling the chief in order to go for a drive. Here, the fire engine supported his idea of being a fireman. Moreover, the existence of the walkie-talkie reminded him to carry out the play action to call the chief. Later when the boys as firemen arrived at the scene of a fire the fire hose and the ladder mediated the play actions: climbing up the ladder and hosing water on the fire.

Because the objects or artefacts mediate the play activity, and with that influence and regulate the play actions and the object of the play, perhaps teachers need to be more conscious of the artefacts in children's play.

Awareness of the importance of artefacts in a frame play means that the teacher should focus on the children's own planning and building up of the physical setting of the play, and with that, the construction of their own artefacts. When the play theme is decided the children talk to each other about possible roles and actions. To continue this, the teacher should support the children as they create equipment and accessories for the play.

There is potential for the children's creation of their own artefacts for the play to have many functions. The visible objects help the children to keep the imaginary play situation, and also will help them to obtain play ideas and to carry them through. In this way, the children will create a many-facetted and complex play environment, which will certainly enrich their play.

Development in conceptualizing transitions

In frame play, teachers and children plan together, and consequently the teachers involve themselves in the play activity. They assume a role and carry out play actions. With reference to Sylva et al. (1980), children are able to maintain their attention and increase the intensity of this attention when adults are present. Wood et al. (1980) also report a positive effect when the adult plays together with the children as a playmate or co-player. The adult achieves a close relationship with the children and a relationship based on trust. In play, the adult has to be sensitive, supporting and avoid being dominant.

In a recent developmental research project, we sought to create an educational play model reflecting the theoretical ideas discussed above, which might bridge preschool and school, informal and formal education, and play and learning. The introduction of such forms of play may serve as tools helping children to cross the boundaries from the activity system of play to the activity system of school learning. In a detailed description (see Broström 2004) the following seven pivotal points could characterize the play context, which should serve as a transitory activity system:

- Reading aloud a short story of high quality literature.
- Based on the story, teacher and children carry through a structured conversation (Chambers 1994) called a *literature dialogue*.
- After the dialogue they *make drawings* to illustrate their understanding of the text.
- From this point of departure the children, in formatted groups, are challenged to turn their literature experiences into *play*. Here, the teacher has an observing role and he/she also participates using the approach 'teacher-in-role'.
- Sometimes the teacher asks them in advance to present their version of their play/story for their classmates and teachers.
- After presentation of the play, the teachers and each play group carry through a structured conversation called a *learning dialogue*.
- During all phases, the teacher and the children have *philosophical dialogues* reflecting their intentions and thoughts expressed in drawings and play activities.

Although we do not describe the children's development of learning motive, one might argue that the combination of reading aloud, literature dialogues and play probably had an influence on the children's learning. Because of the focus of play to continue the themes from the chosen books, and also the focus of presenting the play for their classmates and teachers, the play session crossed the boundaries of what we characterize as free flow play, and Holzman's (1997) idea of interaction of creative imitations and the implementation.

Thus, the transition to school is not only a question of building bridges between settings and arenas. It is a question of developing a new psychological structure in the child's mind, namely the development of the child's learning motive. With reference to Leont'ev (1978, 1981), Enerstvedt (1988) and Pramling (1983), the child goes through a mental transition from '*Play motivation*' towards '*Real motivation for learning*'. In 'play motivation' motivation for learning is integrated into the learning process, and the consciousness of the child's own learning is rather vague. In contrast, a child with 'real motivation for learning' believes that learning is to understand. The child understands learning as a process through which they will understand and realize something; learning as 'access to' being able to do something. That implies a motivation that goes beyond the current situation. In order to obtain such a development, I have suggested that new kinds of expansive play might be a possible method, and with that I have argued for a new concept in the field of transition: play as transitory activity.

References

Aidarova, L. (1982) *Child Development and Education*. Moscow: Progress.

Bateson, G. (1972) *Steps to an Ecology of Mind*. New York: Ballantine Books.

Baumer, S. (2003) Social-cultural 'versus' Activity accounts of motivational development associated with the transition to formal education. Paper presented at the conference of the Society for Research in Child Development, Tampa, Florida, April 24–27.

Baumer, S., Ferholt, B. and Nielsson, M. (2004) *The Playworld of Baba Yaga: a Study of Narrative-based Early Childhood Educational Practice*. Paper presented at the Third Nordic Conference on Cultural Activity Research. 3–5 September Copenhagen.

Broström, S. (1996). Frame play with 6 year old children, *European Early Childhood Education Research Journal*, 4(1): 89–102.

Broström, S. (1997) Children's play: tools and symbols in frame play, *Early Years*, 17(2): 16–21.

Broström, S. (1999a) Changes in early childhood education in Denmark—the appearance of literacy in early childhood education, in G. Brougére and Sylvie Rayna (eds) *Culture, enfance et éducation préscolaire* [*Culture, Childhood and Preschool Education*]. Paris: UNESCO, Université-Nord and INRP.

Broström, S. (1999b) Drama-games with six-year-old children. Possibilities and limitations, in Yrjö Engeström and Raija-Leena Punamaki (eds) *Perspectives on Activity Theory*. New York: Cambridge University Press.

Broström, S. (2001) Constructing the early childhood curriculum: the example of Denmark, in T. David (ed.) *Promoting Evidence-based Practice in Early Childhood Education: Research and its Implications*. London: JAI.

Broström, S. (2002a) Communication and continuity in the transition from kindergarten to school, in H. Fabian and A-W. Dunlop (eds) *Transitions in the*

Early Years. Debating Continuity and Progression for Children in Early Education. London: RoutledgeFalmer.

Broström, S. (2002b) Children Tell Stories, *European Early Childhood Education Research Journal*, 10: 85–97.

Broström, S. (2003a) Transition from kindergarten to school in Denmark: building bridges, in S. Broström and J.T. Wagner (eds) *Early Childhood Education in Five Nordic Countries: Perspectives on the Transition from Preschool to School*. Århus: Systime Academic.

Broström, S. (2003b) Problems and barriers in children's learning when they transit from kindergarten to kindergarten class in school, *European Early Childhood Research Journal, Research Monograph Series*, 1(1): 51–66.

Broström, S. (2004) Frame Play as a Transitory Activity: Danish Experiences. Paper Presented at the American Educational Research Association 12–16 April 2004 San Diego.

Broström, S. (2005) Transition problems and play as transitory activity, *Australian Journal of Early Childhood*. Vol 30. No 3 pp. 17–26

Broström, S. and Wagner, J.T. (2003) *Early Childhood Education in Five Nordic Countries: Perspectives on the Transition from Preschool to School*. Århus: Systime Academic.

Chambers, A. (1994) *Tell Me: Children Reading and Talk*. Stroud: Thimble Press.

Christie, J.F. (1994) Literacy play interventions: a review of empirical research, in S. Reifel (ed.) *Advances in Early Education and Day Care*, Greenwich, CN: JIA Press.

Cole, M. (1990) Cultural psychology: a once and future discipline? in R. A. Dienstbier and J. J. Berman (eds) *Cross-cultural Perspectives*, Nebraska Symposium on Motivation. 1989, Volume 37: 279–335. Lincoln: University of Nebraska Press.

Cole, M., Gay, J., Glick, J. and Sharp, D. (1971) *The Cultural Context of Learning and Thinking—an Exploration in Experimental Anthropology*. New York: Basic Books, Inc. Publishers.

Davydov, V. (1977) *Arten der verallgemeinerung im Unterricht*. Berlin: Volk und Wissen.

Elkonin, D.B. (1980) *Psychologie des Spiels*. Berlin: Volk und Wissen.

Enerstvedt, T.R. (1988) *Barn virksomhet og mening. Utviklingen av læremotivasjon hos norske skolebarn. [Children, Activity, Meaning. Development of Learning Motivation by Norwegian School Children]*. Oslo: Falken Forlag.

Engeström, Y. (1987) *Learning by Expanding. An Activity-theoretical Approach to Development Research*. Helsinki: Orienta-Konsultit.

Fabian, H. and Dunlop, A.W. (2002) Conclusions: debating transitions, continuity and progression in the early years, in H. Fabian and A-W. Dunlop (eds) *Transitions in the Early Years. Debating Continuity and Progression for Children in Early Education*. London: RoutledgeFalmer.

Fine, G.A. (1983) *Shared Fantasy Role-playing Games as Social Worlds*. Chicago: University of Chicago Press.

Garvey, C. (1976) Some properties of social play, in J. Bruner, A. Jolly and K. Sylva (eds) *Play—Its Role in Development and Evolution*. New York: Penguin Books.

Holzman, L. (1997) *Schools for Growth: Radical Alternatives to Current Educational Models*. London: Lawrence Erlbaum.

Lave, J. (1997) Learning, apprenticeship, social practice, *Journal of Nordic Educational Research*, 3: 140–51.

Lave, J. and Wenger, E. (1991) *Situated Learning*. Cambridge: Cambridge University Press.

Leont'ev, A.N. (1978) *Activity, Consciousness and Personality*. Englewood: Prentice Hall, Inc.

Leont'ev, A.N. (1981) *Problems of the Development of the Mind*. Moscow: Progress Publishers.

Lillemyr, O.F. (2001) Play and learning in school. A motivational approach, in D. McInterney and S. Van Etten (eds) *Research on Sociocultural Influences on Motivation and Learning*. Greenwich: Information Age Publishing Inc.

Lindqvist, G. (1995) *The Aesthetic of Play. A Didactic Study of Play and Culture in Preschools*. Göteborg: Coronet books.

Newman, R.F. and Holzman, L. (1993) *Lev Vygotsky: Revolutionary Scientist*. New York: Routledge.

Piaget, J. (1964) *Six etudes de psychologie*. Paris: Gonthier.

Pramling, I. (1983) *The Child's Conception of Learning*. Göteborg: ACTA Universitatis Gotheburgensis.

Rogoff, B. (1990) Apprenticeship in thinking: cognitive development in social context. New York, NY: Oxford University Press.

Shore, R. (1998) *Ready Schools. A Report of the Goal 1 Ready Schools Resource Group*. Washington, DC: National Educational Goals Panel.

Sylva, K., Roy, C. and Painter, M. (1980) *Childwatching at Playgroup and Nursery School*. London: Grant McIntyre.

van der Veer, R. and Valsiner, J. (1991) *Understanding Vygotsky*. Oxford: Basil Blackwell.

Venger, L. (1985) Development of the psychological preparation formal instruction. (Title translated from Russian). *Doshkolnoe Vospitanii*, 7/1985, Moscow.

Vygotsky, L.S. (1978) *Mind in Society*. Cambridge, MA: Harvard University Press.

Vygotsky, L.S. (1985) *Die instrumentelle Methode in der Psychologie*, Ausgewälhlte Schriften Bd. 1. Berlin: Volk und Wissen.

Vygotsky, L.S. (1993) The collective are a factor in the development of abnormal child, in R. W. Rieber and A. S. Carton (eds) *The Collected Works of L. S. Vygotsky*, Vol. 2. New York: Plenum.

Wagner, J.T. (2003) Introduction: international perspectives and Nordic contributions, in S. Broström and J.T. Wagner (eds) *Early Childhood Education in Five Nordic Countries: Perspectives on the Transition from Preschool to School*. Århus: Systime Academic.

Wood, E. and Attfied T.J. (1996) *Play, Learning and the Early Childhood Curriculum*. London: Paul Chapman.

Wood, D., Mcmahon, L. and Cranstoun, Y. (1980) *Working Under Fives*. London: Grant McIntyre.

6 Children's voices on the transition from preschool to primary school

Jóhanna Einarsdóttir

Introduction

In recent years, there has been a growing interest in listening to children's perspectives on matters concerning them and involving them in research. Transition from preschool settings to primary school involves a major change in children's lives and, therefore, listening to children's experiences of and views on this critical period is important. This is a period that can play an important role in the future well being of children and their long-term school success. Research has, for instance, revealed that children who have a difficult time adjusting to school from the beginning, and who experience social, behavioural or academic difficulties in the early years of schooling are more likely to continue experiencing these problems throughout their schooling (Ladd and Price 1987; Love Trudeu and Thayer 1992; Entwisle and Alexander 1998; Kagan and Neuman 1998; Margetts 2002). Adults' views on this period in children's lives have been studied widely; however, in recent years interest in looking at transition to school from children's perspectives has grown. This chapter focuses on children's views on the transition from preschool to primary school deriving from recent research. The chapter starts by discussing the reasons for involving children in research. Attention is then given to critical issues in research with children and appropriate methods to use with children. Transition studies involving children as participants are then examined, summarized and discussed, and the chapter concludes with reflections and implications for further research.

Research with children

The increasing interest in involving children in research and listening to their perspectives derives from a recent evolution in how children and childhood are viewed. From a sociological perspective, childhood is viewed as a social construction and children as already social actors, instead of being in the process of becoming such. Childhood and children are therefore seen as worthy of investigation in their own right, separate from their parents or caregivers (James and Prout 1990; Qvortrup 1994, 2004; Corsaro 1997; Christensen and James 2000; Lloyd-Smith and Tarr 2000; O'Kane 2000). From the postmodern perspective, children are looked upon as knowledgeable, competent, strong and powerful members of society (Bruner 1996; Dahlberg et al. 1999). Hence, children are seen as strong, capable and knowledgeable experts on their own lives, possessing knowledge, perspective and interest that is best gained from themselves (Langsted 1994; Dahl 1995; Mayall 2000; Clark and Moss 2001).

The contemporary children's rights movement also emphasizes taking children seriously and their right to express their own beliefs (Freeman 1998). The *Convention on the Rights of the Child* drawn up by the United Nations in 1989 recognizes the right for children to participate in decisions affecting their lives and communicate their own views. Article 12 of the convention states that parties should ensure that a child who is capable of forming his or her own view should have the right to express these views freely on all matters affecting the child, and that those views should be given weight in accordance with age and maturity (*Convention on the Rights of the Child* 1989). Recent research with children and young people has thus moved from seeing children as dependent and incompetent, that is, as persons acted upon by others, to seeing children as social actors, participants and co-researchers (James and Prout 1990; Christensen and Prout 2002; Lewis 2004). Researchers now talk about research with children instead of research about or on children (Corsaro and Molinari 2000; Mayall 2000; O'Kane 2000; Fraser 2004).

Children's participation in research builds on the belief that children, just like adults, hold their own views and opinions, they have the right to express their ideas, and they are capable of expressing them. Dahlberg et al. (1999), Dahl (1995) and Mayall (2000) point out that children have their own voices and should be listened to and taken seriously. Clark and Moss (2001), and Langsted (1994) consider children as experts on their own lives, and Hennessy (1999) believes that children have a great deal of important information to contribute about themselves. Oldfather (1995) and Alderson (2000) see students as experts on their own perceptions and experiences as learners. Cook-Sather (2002) discussed the importance of authorizing children's perspectives in the critique and reform of education, and Tolfree and Woodhead (1999) see children as powerful social actors, and principal stakeholders who can help shape policy and practice.

Critical issues in research with children

Ethical issues, including informed consent, confidentiality, protection and relationships are fundamental in all research, but in research with children these take on an extra substance.

Good relationships between participants and the researchers are of key importance in qualitative research where the researchers and the participants are in close proximity. Researchers conducting research with children have pointed out that children are potentially more vulnerable to unequal power relationships in research than other groups (Coyne 1998; Balen et al. 2000/ 2001; Punch 2002; Robinson and Kellett 2004). Unequal power can exist in terms of age, status and experience. Children may perceive the adult as an authority figure and consequently may try to please the adult for fear of their reaction if they do not. It can be difficult to elude or even reduce the unequal power relationships between an adult researcher and a child. Meeting the children in their natural contexts, where they feel comfortable, is one way to minimize the power differential, while another way to enable children to feel more at ease with an adult researcher is through child-centred or child-friendly methods and techniques which build on children's competencies and interests (Morrow and Richards 1996; Mauthner 1997; Brooker 2001; Punch 2002; Barker and Weller 2003; Eder and Fingerson 2003). Other authors have suggested that researchers should look at the child as the expert and introduce themselves as a learner who asks the children to be their teacher (Davis 1998; Graue and Walsh 1998).

Informed consent means that participants enter the research project voluntarily, understanding the nature of the study and the danger and obligations that are involved (Bogdan and Biklen 1998). When children are asked to give informed consent they must be given enough information in a language understandable to them to allow them to make an informed decision about participation. It is important that they should know and comprehend the purpose of the research, what the research involves, what is going to happen and for how long, how the results will be used and the consequences of taking part. The children must also be able to understand that participation is voluntary and that they are free to withdraw at any time (Davis 1998; Balen et al. 2000/2001; Parson and Stephenson 2003). With young children, these issues might become problematic for several reasons, the most important being the power inequality between the adult and the child, which can result in the children finding it difficult to tell an adult researcher if they do not want to continue. Alderson (2000) suggested that when children agree to participate in a study, their consent should be open for review during the course of the study. The children should have the power to leave when they want.

Confidentiality in research means that, unless otherwise agreed to, the participants' identities should be protected so that the information collected does not embarrass or in other ways harm them (Bogdan and Biklen 1998). There is a universal agreement that researchers should ensure that the participants are not at risk of becoming hurt, and the confidentiality of all data is a fundamental part of respecting and protecting the participant in any study; the situation is certainly the same when children are involved. Morrow and Richards (1996) have pointed out that children are vulnerable, and the interaction between researcher and child involves power relationships that create an obligation on adults to ensure that children do not suffer harm when participating in research. Nevertheless, researchers working with children have cautioned that researchers should be careful of explicitly promising confidentiality, as this may not always be possible, such as in the case of child abuse when a researcher may need to pass on information to others (Balen et al. 2000/2001; Cree et al. 2002).

Methods in research with children

When conducting research with children, it is important to keep in mind that children are not a homogenous group of people (Christensen and Prout 2002). James and Prout (1990) have pointed out that variety in children's voices should be understood and listened to, and similarly Davis (1998) recognizes that since there are varieties of children's cultures, different children may have contradictory wishes and expectations. Since children are different, researchers also need to be resourceful and use inventive, and original research methods and instruments that suit different children. Graue and Walsh (1998) claim that generating data on children challenges the researcher to be creative, and find new and different ways to listen to and observe children, and this requires constant improvisation. Punch (2002) suggests that one way of researching a diversity of childhoods, and taking into account children's varied social competencies and experiences is to use a range of different methods and techniques. Barker and Weller (2003) talk about children-centred research methods that place the voices of children at the centre of the research process, and are based upon children's preferred methods, of communication. Similarly, Fraser (2004) talks about child-centred or child-friendly methods, where attempts are made to negotiate and understand research aims in terms that make sense to children. She has pointed out that researchers must have a vocabulary and empathy that relate to the child's conception of their world. Negotiations may be necessary, since different children might need different methods. Those negotiations may lead to particular types of child-friendly methods, which have been negotiated between the researcher and the participant.

Researchers have used a range of methods that privilege children as the subjects of research, such as participant observation, focus groups, small group discussion, interviews and structured activities (Mauthner 1997). New methodologies have been developed to allow children to express their beliefs and views through other means than verbal language, for example, art work, drama, music, dance, play, photography and videos (Mauthner 1997; Tolfree and Woodhead 1999; Alderson 2000; Christensen and James 2000).

Participant observations and interviews in one form or another are the most common method used in research with children. Several authors have recommended interviewing children in pairs or groups (Hood 1996; Graue and Walsh 1998; Greig and Taylor 1999; Mayall 2000; Einarsdóttir 2002). The group setting is seen as important for minimizing the power difference between the researcher and the children, and children are more relaxed when with a friend than alone with an adult (Graue and Walsh 1998; Edler and Fingerson 2003). Other researchers have recommended using various props in the interviews, such as toys, paper and crayons, sand, clay, pictures, photographs, dolls, and puppets (Brooker 2001; Doverborg and Pramling Samuelsson 2003).

Children's views on starting school

During the last decade or so, research on children's transitions from preschool to school has increasingly involved children and sought their views. A selection of the literature on children's views on transition from preschool to primary school will be reviewed below and the following questions will be examined:

- How do children experience this critical period?
- What are their concerns, expectations and anticipations?
- What are the commonalities and differences among these studies?
- What data gathering methods were used in these studies?

Nordic studies

In the Nordic countries an emphasis has been placed on taking children's views and rights seriously. In Norway, Sweden and Iceland, children have their own ombudsman and in Denmark an advisory board for children has been established. These are official advocates who ensure that children's voices are heard and correctly understood within the larger society (Broström 2005). Nordic preschools have a child-centred view, where play and free choice is highly valued. Several studies have been conducted in the Nordic countries on children's views on their preschool and school and the differences between these. Broström (2001, 2003) studied Danish children's expectations about school and their fulfilment. The children were interviewed by their teachers in preschool, kindergarten and first grade. When the preschool children were asked what they thought they would do and learn in kindergarten, most of them expressed a school-orientated expectation, such as reading, writing and mathematics, while some children expected a combination of preschool and school emphasis. When the children were asked a year later what they had learned in kindergarten, the results show that most of the children experienced congruence between expectations and fulfilment. At the end of first grade, the children were interviewed again. When they were asked what they found different between kindergarten and first grade, the children in general thought they learned more in grade one, and there was more time and space for play in kindergarten. Although several of them expressed a wish for more play, they were satisfied with first grade. Most of the children said that they had learned what they expected to learn.

Rasmussen and Smidt (2002) studied Danish children's views on their preschool and their primary school. The method of data gathering was children's photographs and interviews concerning the pictures. The results show that the children view preschool and primary school, and the staff in these institutions quite differently. They see the school teacher's work involving direct teaching, while the preschool teachers are more on the sideline, supporting the children. In both institutions, they believe that teachers decide on all activities except for play, where the children are in charge. Friends and other children are most important in preschool and school, and children see play as the most important mode of communicating with other children.

Pramling and Willams-Graneld (1993) used open-ended interviews to interview 7-year-old Swedish children, who had attended first grade for 3 months, about their first experiences in school, and their views of the differences between preschool and school. The result of the study reveals that the children described beginning elementary school with mixed feelings. The positive feelings included learning new things, being in new surroundings and making new friends, but they were also worried about what would be expected of them in school. Concerns included the fear of being lonely, curiosity about the new teacher, fear of the unknown, fear of making mistakes and trepidation about low grades. The greatest difference between preschool and elementary school, according to the children, is that there was more time in preschool for unstructured, freely-chosen activities, such as playing. When the children talked about what they learned in elementary school, they primarily mentioned learning to count, read and write. Everything was more difficult and serious in elementary school, according to them. The children believed that the elementary school stands for the right way of learning and that preschool was training for elementary school. The preschool represents play and free learning, while elementary school represents seriousness and structured learning.

Another Swedish study (Pramling et al. 1995) shows similar results. A group of first grade children were interviewed about their views on the difference between preschool and school. The children regard school as a place where you work, but in preschool you play. They defined play as something that they themselves choose and although they were working at similar subjects that were organized by the teachers, the children did not define it as play because they did not organize and choose for themselves. They felt that they learned the right way in school. The children said that they missed preschool, but they were also positive about school. They took both institutions as given and did not question what happens in either environment.

In Norway, Eide and Winger (1994) interviewed 6-year-old children attending a preschool group within the primary school area, about what they thought they would do in first grade and what other children had told them that they did in school. The results show that the children seemed to have internalized a traditional and stereotypical view of school. Many of them mentioned that in school you would have to sit still, read, do arithmetic, write and do assignments, instead of the playing that took place in preschool. The children had a general idea of the daily routine in the elementary school, and were concerned about the norms and regulations in the school. They mentioned that they had to be aware of certain routines and rules, such as only playing during recess and raising your hand to say something; they seemed to take the rules for granted and did not question them. When they discussed what they would miss from preschool, they mentioned their friends. These children were attending preparatory class for 6-year-olds before starting school and most of them did not seem to worry much about starting school.

Einarsdóttir (2003) investigated Icelandic preschool children's views and attitudes concerning their transition into primary school. Group interviews were conducted with 5- and 6-year-old children during the end of their last year at preschool. The results show that many of the children had the image of school as a place where children sat quietly at their desks learning how to read, write and do mathematics. The children were preoccupied with the ways in which the primary school would be different from preschool. They also saw learning the customs of the school, the school rules and how to behave in school as an important part of what they would be learning in first grade. Many of the children were excited and looked forward to starting school, while others worried about not being able to meet the school's expectations.

Other European studies

Corsaro and Molinari (2000) studied preschool children in an Italian pre-school and followed them when they started elementary school. Ethno-graphic methods were employed where the researchers carefully entered and participated daily, for a 5-month period in the preschool, for 4 months at the beginning of the school term in first grade and for a 1-week period during the end of the school year. The preschool children viewed elementary school as more work- than play-focused, and saw their abilities to read and write as important in their forthcoming transition to elementary school. The children also expected that they would not play as much in the first grade as they had in preschool and that they would have to work quietly at their desks. The importance of older siblings was evident and the children often referred to the experiences of older siblings. When the children entered first grade, they discovered that time was differentiated into time periods more strictly than in preschool. For example, different parts of the school day were signalled by ringing bells. They also found a sharp dichotomy between work and play that had not existed in the preschool. The lack of play-time was one of the chil-dren's major concerns, as was the large number of new rules. The children made a generally smooth transition to elementary school. In regard to ad-justment to new rules and schedules, to more highly structured lessons, and to maintaining and expanding friendship, the results revealed that the chil-dren's collective experiences in priming events in the preschool provided insights enabling them to anticipate and accomplish the transition.

Griebel and Niesel (2002) studied how German children coped with entry into kindergarten. Interviews were conducted with children at the end of the last year in preschool, and 3 and 6 months after entry into school. The results show that all the children were looking forward to school, although some seemed a little anxious about what would come. Their knowledge about what school meant was vague and they did not report much concrete information even if they had visited school with their preschool class. All the children were convinced that they would do well at school, were supported by parents and their preschool teachers, and they were not afraid that older children might bully them. After they had attended school for some weeks, they felt that entering school was somewhat different from what they had expected. They were overwhelmed by many new impressions, such as the large number of other children in their classroom and in school, and they had learned that they were told to do things instead of choosing things as in preschool. How-ever, the children enjoyed learning new things and they felt supported by the teacher. Half a year later, the children in general had turned out to be com-petent school children. They had acquainted themselves with school demands and made friends. Nevertheless, they felt homework to be a burden, and said that they wanted fewer school hours and more free time in the morning.

Asian studies

In contrast to the Nordic countries, Singapore has a highly competitive education system where competition and extrinsic rewards for achievement in school feature strongly even at an early age (Clarke and Sharpe 2003). In a recent study, a group of 6-year-old children were interviewed about their transition from preschool to formal schooling. In the first week of school, each child had a fifth grade child acting as his or her chaperone during recess time. Five months later, the children took part in a structured interview by their friends who had previously been trained. The results show that almost all the children had made new friends, and enjoyed the larger school building and facilities. They held a very serious view of schooling, where learning was centre stage and play took a back seat. They registered a positive view of themselves as learners. Many were concerned about school rules. While the majority did not indicate anxieties about school, some expressed worries that pertained mostly to being reprimanded by teachers, the principal and vice principal (Clarke et al. in press).

In Hong Kong, parents, teachers and children expressed their views of transition to school (Chun 2003). The children were interviewed in groups a month after they started primary school and again at the end of the school year. Most of the children said that they were happy at school. In the first interview, most of them mentioned that they liked having recess best, playing with classmates and learning new things. A few also mentioned that they liked the enhanced status of being a primary school pupil. The things they did not like were the English lessons and being punished. Nearly all the children said that they preferred the primary school over the kindergarten. In the second interview, although most of the children liked primary school, some children (typically the low achievers) wanted to go back to kindergarten because there was no homework and no examinations in kindergarten. However, most of the children said they liked the primary school because they enjoyed playing with classmates, the PE lessons, the recess, the opportunity to learn more and studying in an upper grade.

Studies in Australia and New Zealand

In Australia, the Starting School Project has investigated children's transition to school for a number of years. As a part of that study, informal group interviews were conducted with children who had recently started school, who were about to start school and who had been at school for some time. The interview transcripts were analysed according to the following categories: knowledge, adjustment, skills, dispositions, rules, physical, family issues and educational environment. The categories of rules and dispositions predominated. Dispositions about school were often associated with friends and, for many children, liking school involved making friends and being with those friends. The children emphasized that they needed to know the school rules in order to function well within the school and keep out of trouble, and they were very clear that the rules came from the teachers. Children also mentioned physical issues in starting school, such as the size of the school, the physical nature of play and the playground at school. Many showed concern about the big kids and the scary nature of interactions with them. Several children indicated that some knowledge was required to start school, such as knowing how to count, knowing your name and knowing how to read, but few children mentioned skills such as being able to colour properly or write all the letters of their name (Dockett and Perry 2002, 2004). In the Starting School Research Project children's photos were also used for gathering data (Dockett and Perry 2003). The children were asked to photograph what they though kindergarten children need to know when they start school. As in previous studies, the children often spoke about the rules they needed to know in order to manage the school environment, they took photos of things related to everyday routines and functioning in the classroom, the physical environment, such as the actual classroom and the teacher's chair, the play area, merit charts and the computer. Other areas of interest were the playground, toilets and specific function areas such as the library.

In another study of Australian children and their families' views on transition from childcare to school, Elliott (1998) interviewed children on two occasions when they made the transition to school; the first interview was 2–3 months preceding the transition, the second 2–3 months into the new school year. Results of the study show generally positive transition experiences of the children. In the first interview, the children were excited about the prospect of attending school and were well informed about what would happen there, such as that they would learn to read and count, and do 'proper' drawing. At the same time, some children had a very strong sense of attachment to the childcare centre and individual staff. In the second interview that took place after the children started school, all the children found the day-to-day experiences of school very positive. The children recalled feeling both excited and apprehensive about starting school. The author comments that all the children had attended good quality childcare, had participated in varying activities designed to prepare them for school and went to a school where they knew other children.

As a part of a large study on how children aged 5–9 years perceived their world, a group of 100 Australian children aged 5–6 years were questioned about their early experiences of school. The children were interviewed individually, using an interview schedule consisting of 100 multiple choice and open question. The results indicate that, while most children settle well in school, many have concerns about the affective domain of the school environment, the fear of punishment, being bored and the lack of choice. While just over half of the children like school most of the time, 83% of them said they did not like school work (Potter and Briggs 2003).

Peters (2000) examined transition experiences of young children, their families, and their early childhood and primary school teachers in New Zealand. Seven case study children were interviewed and observed in kindergarten and first grade. The results reveal that for many of the children, the lack of continuity between kindergarten and elementary school was temporarily unsettling. This was reflected in a number of aspects, including the physical environment, the size of the school buildings and grounds, the number and size of the other children, the length of the day and the demands of the curriculum. They noted that there was less freedom of choice at school, compared with their experiences in kindergarten. The children also mentioned the compulsion to follow routines for work and for play, regardless of what they felt like doing. The children disliked not being able to play when they wanted, having outside time restricted, not having access to resources such as art materials, and being told what to do all the time. The results of the study indicate that, although aspects of discontinuity provided a challenge for the children on entry to school, in general they adapted quickly to the new environment and the demands of the new curriculum, and showed pride in their achievements. The author concluded that, although discontinuities in the children's experiences as they move from early childhood to school can be a source of distress for young children, discontinuity was also associated with delight in learning new things.

Ledger et al. (1998) studied how children in New Zealand viewed their transition to school. They followed a group of children from preschool to school using participant observations and interviews with the children at home, in their early childhood centre and in school. The findings show that the children had unrealistic expectations about what would happen at school and some became very negative about school soon after they started. Moving from preschool, where they could initiate their own learning, and control their interactions with peers and teachers, to a school environment, where they experienced much more teacher direction, presented problems for some of the children.

A study from the United States

In the United States, Seefeldt et al. (1997) interviewed Head Start children about their conceptions of and expectations for their future schooling. An open-end questionnaire designed to engage children in a dialogue about their understanding of school was used when the children were interviewed. The children who participated in the study included children at the end of their Head Start year and children who were already in kindergarten. Two major themes in children's conceptions of school emerged: play, and the cognitive or learning environment. Children realistically talked about the work of school becoming less play centred, more difficult, and more centred on academics as they moved from grade to grade. Some of the children saw this change as normal, and accepted it on the grounds that, as they grew and matured, they would be able to meet the increased demands. In another study on Head Start children's perspectives about school and the transition to school, a group of children were interviewed after their transition to kindergarten (Ramey et al. 1998). Most of the children had positive perceptions of all aspects of school. However, a subset of children, more often boys, reported they did not like school very much and were not doing well.

Summary and conclusion

The review of the literature on children's views on transition from preschool to primary school renders some common factors that children see characterizing these school levels and they find they have to be aware of for a successful transition. Irrespective of country of residence, the children expect a change from being able to play and choose in preschool to more academic work in the primary school. They are also aware of that there are new rules and norms that they have to learn and adapt to. For them, that is the nature of school and they do not question it. Many of the studies reveal that other children and friends are very important during this period and the children report that they will miss the children that do not accompany them to school. Many children also report that they will miss playing in the preschool. The studies conducted after the children started primary school reveal that children often experience a setback and feel inferior during the first weeks or months in school, but most of them seem to adapt quickly. Although there are many commonalities among the research results reviewed, there are also some differences and exceptions. For instance, the children in some of the studies did not worry at all about starting school (Eide and Winger 1994), while children in other studies had mixed feelings about starting school (Einarsdóttir 2003; Pramling Samuelsson and Willams-Graneld 1993). Similarly, whereas the children in one study (Ledger et al. 1998) had unrealistic expectations about school, children in other studies had realistic views of school and when they came to school they were doing what they had expected (Broström 2001, 2003).

Nevertheless, the results of the studies reviewed indicate that most preschool children see starting school as a period of big change in their lives. They expect their days of playing to be over, and they have to take on new tasks and new ways when they start primary school. In most countries, preschools and primary schools have different traditions, policies, curriculum, teaching methodologies, environment and surroundings (Fabian and Dunlop 2002; Broström and Wagner 2003), and the children have been prepared for this change by their social environment, including their preschools, older children and their parents.

One of the interpretations of these results is that children's perspectives reflect cultural views. From a sociocultural perspective, cultural context plays an important role in shaping children's views. Bruner (1996) has, for example, pointed out the importance of culture in shaping the human mind and argued that children have a strong 'disposition to culture' (47) since they are sensitive to and eager to adopt the ways of people they encounter around them. In a similar manner, Rogoff (1993) discusses the concept of apprenticeship, and suggests that children's social interactions and involvement in activities are dynamic and inseparable from the cultural context, in which children engage in shared thinking, as well as comparison of ideas with other people that vary in age, skills and status. Graue and Walsh (1998) explain that children cannot remain untouched by their contexts, and that young children especially are more context dependent and context vulnerable than older children and adults. Therefore, children should be studied as members of social systems and as historically and culturally situated as has been pointed out by other researchers (Saljö 1991).

It is also important to keep in mind when looking at these research results that children are not a homogenous group of people (Christensen and Prout 2002), and different children may have contradictory wishes, expectations and perspectives. Although most of the children in the studies reported that they looked forward to school and adapted quickly, this might not be the case with all children. When conducting research with children, a variety of children's voices should be listened to (James and Prout 1990). Therefore, researchers need to be resourceful, use creative research methods and instruments that suit different children, and take into account children's varied social competencies and experiences (Morrow and Richards 1996; Mauthner 1997; Graue and Walsh 1998; Brooker 2001; Punch 2002; Barker and Weller 2003; Eder and Fingerson 2003). The most common method used in the studies reviewed in this chapter was the interview in one form or another. Perhaps these methods do not fit all children, and do not take into consideration the interests and strong points of all children, or their preferred methods of communication. Group interviews have been reported as having many advantages with young children (Hood 1996; Graue and Walsh 1998; Greig and Taylor 1999; Mayall 2000; Einarsdóttir 2002), but they also have limitations and might possibly only capture the voices of some children. The voices of children with limited language skills, and children with special needs, for instance, might not be heard during group interviews. One consideration for further research on children's perspectives on the transition to school is to keep in mind that there is diversity among children and varieties of children's voices to be heard. To be able to capture different children's perspectives and give their views weight as the *Convention on the Rights of the Child* (1989) stipulates, we need to meet children on their own premises, in their natural context, using diverse methods that fit different children.

References

Alderson, P. (2000) Children as researchers. The effect on participation rights on research methodology, in P. Christensen and A. James (eds) *Research with Children*. New York: Falmer Press.

Balen, R., Holroyd, C., Mountain, G., and Wood, B. (2000/2001) Giving children a voice: methodological and practical implications of research involving children, *Paediatric Nursing*, 12(10): 24–9.

Barker, J. and Weller, S. (2003) 'Is it fun?' Developing children centered research methods, *International Journal of Sociology and Social Policy*, 1(2): 33–58.

Bogdan, R. and Biklen, S.K. (1998) *Qualitative Research in Education: An Introduction to Theory and Methods*. Boston: Allyn and Bacon.

Brooker, L. (2001) Interviewing children, in M. G. Naughton, S. Rolfe and I. Siraj-Blatchford (eds) *Doing Early Childhood Research: International Perspectives on Theory and Practice*. Buckingham: Open University Press.

Broström, S. (2001) *Jeg gar i förste! Fra börnehave til hörnehaveklasse of til 1. klasse* [*I am from Grade One! From Preschool to Kindergarten Class and then to Grade One*], report. Copenhagen: Danmarks Pædagogiske Universitet.

Broström, S. (2003) Transition from kindergarten to school in Denmark: building bridges, in S. Broström and J. Wagner (eds) *Early Childhood Education in Five Nordic Countries: Perspectives on the Transition from Preschool to School*. Arhus: Systime/Academic.

Broström, S. (2005) Children's perspectives on their childhood experiences, in J. Einarsdóttir and J. Wagner (eds) *Nordic Childhoods and Early Education: Philosophy, Research, Policy, and Practice in Denmark, Finland, Iceland, Norway, and Sweden*. Connecticut: Information Age.

Broström, S. and Wagner, J. (2003) *Early Childhood Education in Five Nordic Countries: Perspectives on the Transition from Preschool to School*. Arhus: Systime/Academic.

Bruner, J. (1996) *The Culture of Education*. Cambridge, MA: Harvard University Press.

Christensen, P. and James, A. (2000) Researching children and childhood: cultures of communication, in P. Christensen and A. James (eds) *Research with Children*. New York: Falmer Press.

Christensen, P. and Prout, A. (2002) Working with ethical symmetry in social research with children, *Childhood*, 9(4): 477–97.

Chun, W.N. (2003) A study of children's difficulties in transition to school in Hong Kong, *Early Child Development and Care*, 173(1): 83–96.

Clark, A. and Moss, P. (2001) *Listening to Young Children*. London: National Children's Bureau and Rowntree Foundation.

Clarke, C. and Sharpe, P. (2003) Transition from preschool to primary school: an overview of the personal experiences of children and their parents in Singapore. *European Early Childhood Education Research Journal*, Themed monograph series 1: 15–24.

Clarke, C., See, Y.L. and Sharpe, P. (2005) Starting school—a Singapore story told by children, *Australian Journal of Early Childhood* Vol 30 No 3 pp.1–9.

Convention on the Rights of the Child. (1989) Available at: http://www.unhchr.ch/html/menu3/b/k2crc.htm (accessed 31 January 2005).

Cook-Sather, A. (2002) Authorizing students' perspectives: toward trust, dialogue, and change in education, *Educational Researcher*, 31(4): 3–14.

Corsaro, W.A. (1997) *The Sociology of Childhood*. Thousand Oaks: Pine Forge Press.

Corsaro, W.A. and Molinari, L. (2000) Entering and observing in children's worlds: a reflection on a longitudinal ethnography of early education in Italy, in P. Christensen and A. James (eds) *Research with Children*. New York: Falmer Press.

Coyne, I.T. (1998) Researching children: some methodological and ethical considerations, *Journal of Clinical Nursing*, 7: 409–16.

Cree, V., Kay, H. and Tisdall, K. (2002) Research with children: sharing the dilemmas, *Child and Family Social Work*, 7: 47–56.

Dahl, K.L. (1995) Challenges in understanding the learner's perspective, *Theory into Practice. Learning from Student Voices*, 34(2): 124–30.

Dahlberg, G., Moss, P. and Pence, A.R. (1999) *Beyond Quality in Early Childhood Education and Care: Postmodern Perspectives*. London and Philadelphia, PA: Falmer Press.

Davis, J.M. (1998) Understanding the meanings of children: a reflexive process, *Children and Society*, 12: 325–35.

Dockett, S. and Perry, B. (2002) Who's ready for what? Young children starting school, *Contemporary Issues in Early Childhood*, 3(1): 67–89.

Dockett, S. and Perry, B. (2003) Children's voices in research on starting school. Paper presented at the Annual Conference of the European Early Childhood Education Research Association, Glasgow, 3–6 September.

Dockett, S. and Perry, B. (2004) Starting school: perspectives of Australian children, parents and educators, *Journal of Early Childhood Research*, 2(2): 171–89.

Doverborg, E. and Pramling Samuelsson, I. (2003) *Å forstå børns tanker: Børneinterview som pædagogisk redskab* [*To Understand Children's Thinking. Children's Interviews as Pedagogical Tool*] (A. G. Holtough, Trans.). København: Hans Reitzel Forlag.

Eder, D. and Fingerson, L. (2003) Interviewing children and adolescents, in J.A. Holstein and J. Gubrium, F. (eds) *Inside Interviewing: New Lenses, New Concerns*. London: SAGE.

Eide, B. and Winger, N. (1994) *Du gleder deg vel til å begynne på skolen!* [*Aren't You Looking Forward to Starting School!*]. Oslo: Barnevernsakademet.

Einarsdóttir, J. (2002) Children's accounts of the transition from preschool to elementary school, *Barn*, 4: 49–72.

Einarsdóttir, J. (2003) When the bell rings we have to go inside: Preschool children's views on the primary school, *European Early Childhood Education Research Journal*, Themed Monograph Series 1: 35–50.

Elliott, A. (1998) From child care to school: experience and perceptions of children and their families, *Australian Journal of Early Childhood*, 23(3): 26–32.

Entwisle, D.R. and Alexander, K.L. (1998) Facilitating the transition to first grade: the nature of transition and research on factors affecting it, *Elementary School Journal*, 98(4): 351–64.

Fabian, H. and Dunlop, A-W. (eds) (2002) *Transitions in the Early Years: Debating Continuity and Progression for Children in Early Education*. London: Routledge/Falmer.

Fraser, S. (2004) Situating empirical research, in S. Fraser, V. Lewis, S. Ding, M. Kellett and C. Robinson (eds) *Doing Research with Children and Young People*. London: SAGE.

Freeman, M. (1998) The sociology of childhood and children's rights, *International Journal of Children's Rights*, 6: 433–44.

Graue, E.M. and Walsh, D.J. (1998) *Studying Children in Context: Theories, Methods and Ethics*. Thousand Oaks, CA: SAGE.

Greig, A. and Taylor, J. (1999) *Doing Research with Children*. Thousand Oaks, CA: SAGE.

Griebel, W. and Niesel, R. (2002) Co-constructing transition into kindergarten and school by children, parents and teachers, in A-W. Dunlop and H. Fabian (eds) *Transitions in the Early Years: Debating Continuity and Progression for Children in Early Education*. London: Routledge/Falmer.

Hennessy, E. (1999) Children as service evaluators, *Child Psychology and Psychiatry Review*, 4(4): 153–61.

Hood, S. (1996). Children as research subjects: a risky enterprise, *Children and Society*, 10(2): 117–28.

James, A. and Prout, A. (1990) *Constructing and Reconstructing Childhood: Contemporary Issues in Sociological Study of Childhood*. London: Falmer.

Kagan, S.L. and Neuman, M.J. (1998) Lessons from three decades of transition research, *Elementary School Journal*, 98(4): 365–80.

Ladd, J.M. and Price, K. (1987). Predicting children's social and school adjustment following the transition from preschool to kindergarten, *Child Development*, 58(5): 1168–89.

Langsted, O. (1994) Looking at quality from the child's perspective, in P. Moss and A. Pence (eds) *Valuing Quality in Early Childhood Service: New Approaches to Defining Quality*. London: Paul Chapman.

Ledger, E., Smith, A.B. and Rich, P. (1998) Do I go to school to get a brain? The transition from kindergarten to school from the child's perspective, *Children's Issues*, 2(2): 7–11.

Lewis, V. (2004) Doing research with children and young people: an introduction, in S. Fraser, V. Lewis, S. Ding, M. Kellett and C. Robinson (eds) *Doing Research with Children and Young People*. London: SAGE.

Lloyd-Smith, M. and Tarr, J. (2000) Researching children's perspectives: a sociological dimension, in A. Lewis and G. Lindsey (eds) *Researching Children's Perspectives*. Buckingham: Open University Press.

Love, J.M., Trudeu and Thayer. (1992) *Transitions to Kindergarten in American Schools: Final Report of the National Transition Study*, Contract No. LC 88089001. Portsmouth, NH: US Department of Education.

Margetts, K. (2002) Transition to school—complexity and diversity, *European Early Childhood Education Research Journal*, 10(2): 103–14.

Mauthner, M. (1997) Methodological aspects of collecting data from children: lessons from three research projects, *Children and Society*, 11: 16–28.

Mayall, B. (2000) Conversations with children: working with generational issues, in P. Christensen and A. James (eds) *Research with Children: Perspectives and Practices*. New York: Falmer Press.

Morrow, V. and Richards, M. (1996) The ethics of social research with children: an overview, *Children and Society*, 10: 90–105.

O'Kane, C. (2000) The development of participatory techniques. Facilitating children's views about decisions which affect them, in P. Christensen and A. James (eds) *Research with Children: Perspectives and Practices*. New York: Falmer Press.

Oldfather, P. (1995) Songs 'Come back most to them': students' experiences as researchers, *Theory into Practice. Learning from Student Voices*, 34(2): 131–7.

Parson, M. and Stephenson, M. (2003) Giving children a voice: research rights and responsibilities. Paper presented at the European Early Childhood Research Conference, Glasgow, September.

Peters, S. (2000) Multiple perspectives on continuity in early learning and the transition to school. Paper presented at the European Early Childhood Research Conference, London, August 29–September 1, 2000.

Potter, G. and Briggs, F. (2003) Children talk about their early experiences at school, *Australian Journal of Early Childhood*, 28(3): 44–9.

Pramling, I., Klerfelt, A. and Graneld, W. (1995) *Först var det roligt, sen blev det tråkigt och sen vande man sig: Barns möte med skolans värld [First it was Fun, then it Became Boring and then You Got Used to it: Children's Meeting with the World of School]*, Rapport nr. 9. Göteborg: Institutionen för metodik, Göteborg Universitet.

Pramling Samuelsson, I. and Willams-Graneld, P. (1993) Starting compulsory school: preschool teachers' conceptions and children's experience. Paper presented at the OMEP Asia-Pacific Region International Conference, Osaka, Japan.

Punch, S. (2002) Research with children: the same or different from research with adults? *Childhood*, 9(3): 321–41.

Qvortrup, J. (1994) *Explorations in Sociology of Childhood*. Köbenhavn: Sociologisk Institut Köbenhavns Universitet.

Qvortrup, J. (2004) Editorial: the waiting child, *Childhood*, 11(3): 267–73.

Ramey, S.L., Lanzi, R.G., Martha, P. and Ramey, C. (1998) Perspectives of former Head Start children and their parents on school and the transition to school, *Elementary School Journal*, 98(4): 311–27.

Rasmussen, K. and Smidt, S. (2002) *Barndom i billeder: Börns fotografier set som ytringer om en kultur i bevægelse* [*Childhood in Pictures: Children's Photographs as Comments on a Culture in Motion*]. Danmark: Akademisk.

Robinson, C. and Kellett, M. (2004) Power, in S. Fraser, A. Lewis, S. Ding, M. Kellett and C. Robinson (eds) *Doing Research with Children and Young People*. London: SAGE.

Rogoff, B. (1993) Children's guided participation and participatory appropriation in sociocultural activity, in R. H. Wozniak and K. W. Fischer (eds) *Development in Context: Acting and Thinking in Specific Environments*. New Jersey: Lawrence Erlbaum.

Saljö, R. (1991) Introduction: culture and Learning, *Learning and Instruction*, 1: 179–85.

Seefeldt, C., Galper, A. and Denton, K. (1997) Head start children's conceptions of and expectations for their future schooling, *Early Childhood Research Quarterly*, 12: 387–406.

Tolfree, D. and Woodhead, M. (1999) Tapping a key resource, *Early Childhood Matters*, 91: 19–23.

7 Children's transition to school: changing expectations

Sue Dockett and Bob Perry

This chapter explores some of the changes in experiences and expectations that children encounter as they start school. As well as the anticipated changes in curriculum, children experience environments at school that are quite different from the environments of childcare, preschool or home. When considering issues of continuity and discontinuity of curriculum, this chapter takes a broad view of curriculum, encompassing things that happen over a school day, rather than only the planned sequences of learning and teaching. From this broad perspective, we consider 'other' aspects of the school day, such as arrival and departure procedures, playground interactions and learning the school culture as part of the curriculum. The implications of moving from a prior-to-school setting—such as childcare, preschool or home—to school are considered. The major focus is on the changing demands of children, particularly relating to the independence they are expected to demonstrate in school settings.

Introduction

School is a familiar place for most adults and even more familiar for most educators. For children who have not yet started school or those who have only recently started school, much is unfamiliar and unexplained. Roger McGough (n.d.) reminds us of some of the elements in his poem '*First day at school*'.

> *First day at school*
> A millionbillionwillion miles from home
> Waiting for the bell to go. (To go where?)
> Why are they all so big, other children?
> So noisy? So much at home they
> must have been born in uniform.
> Lived all their lives in playgrounds.

Spent the years inventing games
that don't let me in. Games
that are rough, that swallow you up.

And the railings.
All around, the railings.
Are they to keep out wolves and monsters?
Things that carry off and eat children?
Things you don't take sweets from?
Perhaps they're to stop us getting out.
Running away from the lessins. Lessin.
What does a lessin look like?
Sounds small and slimy.
They keep them in glassrooms.
Whole rooms made out of glass. Imagine.

I wish I could remember my name.
Mummy said it would come in useful.
Like wellies. When there's puddles.
Yellowwellies. I wish she was here.
I think my name is sewn on somewhere.
Perhaps the teachers will read it for me.
Tea-cher. The one who makes the tea.

Background

In New South Wales, Australia, children start school at the beginning of the school year, which is in late January. The first compulsory year of school is called Kindergarten. Children attend school for five full days each week. Schools have a Kindergarten to Year 6 curriculum that focuses on traditional subject areas. While it is possible that teachers of the first years of school hold early childhood teaching qualifications, this is not often the case. Most often, Kindergarten teachers are primary trained teachers, who teach across the grades Kindergarten to Year 6.

Children who turn 5 years of age by July 31 are eligible to start school at the beginning of the year. There is only one intake of children each year. The age by which children must be in school is 6 years. Consequently, it is possible that children aged 4 years 6 months will be starting school and going into the same classes, at the same time as children who are 6 years old.

It is also possible that some children aged 4 years 6 months will remain in childcare or preschool services until the following school year. In New South Wales (NSW), two different government departments administer early childhood provision. Prior-to-school services, such as childcare or preschool, operate under the auspices of the Department of Community Services (DoCS), which has the authority to license and regulate services. The Department of Community Services has recently published a curriculum framework for children's services that focuses on relationship building and supporting diversity within the early childhood years [New South Wales Department of Community Services (NSW DoCS) 2002]. The adoption of this curriculum framework is not mandatory. Public schools in NSW operate through the NSW Department of Education and Training (DET). State developed syllabi are used in all public schools. These draw on an outcomes-based approach to education across six key learning areas (English; Mathematics; Science and Technology; Human Society and It's Environment; Personal Development, Health and Physical Education; Creative Arts) (Board of Studies, NSW 2000).

The approaches to curriculum in each of the prior-to-school and school contexts are quite different, both in terms of the organization of teaching and learning, and in the content focus. In general, there is little curriculum continuity across prior-to-school and school settings. Most teachers in the respective settings do not regard this as a problem, preferring to see what happens at school as quite distinct from what happens in prior-to-school settings, commenting that *'school should not be the same as preschool and preschool should not be the same as school'* (Dockett and Perry 2002).

One of the prompts for this chapter was an exploration of what is different for children who could be the same age, but in quite different settings. If the children are much the same, how do the settings differ and what are the expectations of the children in these settings? While most parents and educators, and certainly children, expect there to be differences in curriculum (Dockett and Perry 2004a), little emphasis has been placed on the differences children encounter in the environment (Dunlop 2004), both physical and social. This chapter explores some of the continuities and discontinuities experienced as children move from prior-to-school settings, such as preschool, childcare or home environments, to school.

Continuities and discontinuities

Fabian (2002) described three categories of discontinuity between home or prior-to-school settings and school:

- Physical discontinuities, where the physical surroundings are very different in size, location, the number of people and the like;
- Social discontinuities, where children's identity changes, as does their social network and the adults with whom they interact;

- Philosophical discontinuities, where the approach to learning and teaching can be quite different from that experienced previously.

The discontinuities discussed in this chapter cross these categories, emphasizing the expectations of adults for children to be able to recognize and manage the change they encounter at school. In previous investigations into what matters as children start school, we have reported the expectation that it is the children who will change, as they adapt to the school environment. It is children, more than adults, who are expected to change in terms of knowledge and skills, understanding the rules, adjusting to the physical contexts of the school, accepting the educational environment of the school, and whose disposition and adjustment often signal a positive—or negative—start to school (Dockett et al. 2002).

Pianta (2004) has highlighted four significant areas of change between home or prior-to-school setting and school:

- There is a shift in the academic demands of children. Many children are expected to engage in tasks that may be unfamiliar to them, and their performance on these tasks is used to compare children and make educational decisions.
- The social environment of school is much more complex than that of home or prior-to-school setting. Not only are there many more peers to interact with, as well as a wider range and greater number of children overall, interaction patterns with adults are different from those in other settings.
- There is less parent support in the day-to-day activities of school than in either home or prior-to-school settings. Parents can feel less engaged with school and children can feel that parents are less involved.
- There is less time in school for individual attention from the teacher. Even with small classes, the decrease in staff: child ratios means that teachers have less time to respond on an individual level.

Pianta's (2004) summary of the transition to school is that this is a time when 'the demands go up and the supports go down'. This chapter explores some of the ways the context of school impacts on adult expectations of children, as well as children's expectations of themselves.

Children's perspectives on continuity and discontinuity

It is important to note that the children themselves recognize the differences between school and prior-to-school settings, but they do not necessarily see these as problematic. Rather, they expect school to be different and generally, see this as positive. They are keen to become 'big kids' and going to school is one recognition of their improved status.

Children expect there to be differences in the curriculum of school and prior-to-school settings. Informal discussions with children about to start school and children who have recently started school indicate that they have definite views and expectations of such differences. These discussions have been undertaken in prior-to-school, as well as school settings, in a informal, small group context where children have been invited to talk about going to school.

Generally, children expect to learn more at school and play more at preschool (Dockett and Perry 2004a). They expect to 'work' at school and often expect that this work will be 'hard', as indicated in this discussion with children about to start school:

> *What kind of work (will you do at school)?*
> *Mark:*   Hard work. What's 100 + 100—I know, it's 200!
> *Cassie:*   We have to do homework, but we have to read in class.
> *Mark:*   You have to do hard plusses.
> *Jamie:*   You have to do homework.
>
> (Dockett and Perry 2004a: 17)

Children also realize that the social elements of school will be different from home or prior-to-school settings. Sometimes, it's a matter of 'making sure you don't call the teacher Mum', and other times, it's a matter of recognizing that there will be many different people at school, including 'big kids' (Dockett and Perry 1999a) or knowing that at school 'you can't bring your favourite toy' (Dockett and Perry 2004a: 18).

The school environment holds both challenges and excitement for most children starting school. There is a sense that everything at school is 'big', including the playground, and that this opens up opportunities for play that are not possible in prior-to-school settings or at home. The size of school can, however, be overwhelming, with some children reporting being scared of getting lost of not knowing where to go (Dockett and Perry 1999a).

Expectations that children will manage change

In a major investigation of what is important to different groups of people (children, parents, educators) as children start school, we asked the adult participants to list the first five things that came to mind when they thought of children starting school (Dockett et al. 2002; Dockett and Perry 2004b). Using a grounded theory approach, the frequency, source and strength of responses were recorded, leading to the identification of a series of response categories (Perry et al. 2000). Key among these categories (see Dockett and Perry 1999b) were:

- knowledge;
- social adjustment;
- organizational adjustment;
- skills;
- dispositions;
- rules.

These categories were later refined through factor analysis (Meredith et al. 1999), with the two adjustment categories being combined. Of significance for the discussion in this chapter are responses from 298 parents and 280 teachers (in both prior-to-school and school settings). The parents generated 711 responses that could be coded as one of the six key categories listed above. Similarly, the teachers generated 834 responses in these six categories. Initial coding of responses determined the subject of the comment, for example, within the category of knowledge, whether reference made to children's knowledge, parents' knowledge or teachers' knowledge. Table 1 lists the number of responses relating to children, from teachers and parents for these categories. (Responses relating to parents and teachers are not included in this table, with the result that the figures listed do not equal 100%.)

Table 1. Distribution of responses from parents and teachers across six key categories

Category participant group	Parent response		Teacher response	
	Number (n = 711)	Percentage of total	Number (n = 834)	Percentage of total
Knowledge—children	17	2	50	6
Social adjustment—children	270	38	288	36
Organizational adjustment—children	110	15	122	15
Skills—children	52	7	151	18
Disposition—children	134	19	134	16
Rules—children	57	8	27	3

Perhaps not surprisingly, adults thought of children and the changes they would need to make as they started school. While this may not be surprising, it is notable that neither parents nor teachers regarded themselves as having to change as much as the children during the transition to school (Dockett et al. 2002). In general, as children start school there is a clear expectation that they will change, and change considerably. In other words, the expectation is that the least experienced participants in the transition—children—will change the most.

There are some indications from Table 1 about the nature of expected change. While there is some focus from the adults on children's knowledge and skills, these represent only 2 and 7%, respectively, of the responses. Attracting much more focus are other aspects of children's transition to school—their social adjustment, their ability to fit in to the organization of school, their understanding of the rules of school and their emotional response to school. Some of the areas highlighted by adults, as well as children are the basis of the following discussion.

Changes in expectations

Duty of care

Parents have commented on the changed expectations for their children in a wide range of areas (Dockett and Perry 2004b). One consistent issue comes under the heading of duty of care, with parents asking 'Will anyone check that my child eats lunch, washes their hands before eating, drinks regularly?' Generally, teachers in schools do not see these as part of their roles, although many teachers of children in their first year at school do offer reminders, at least early in the school year.

Some contrasts between prior-to-school or home settings are noticeable when considering eating arrangements generally. Children in early childhood settings/homes generally sit indoors, in small groups, often with an adult, and have interesting conversations at meal times. Children at school generally sit together in large groups with limited adult supervision or interaction. In some schools, large shaded outdoor areas are provided for children to sit and eat lunch. In other schools, there are fewer shaded places to eat. In NSW schools, children bring their lunch to school or purchase lunch from the school canteen. On all possible occasions, lunch is eaten outside in the playground. Often there is pressure (whether real or perceived) for them to eat quickly so that they can go and play with their friends.

The timing of lunch can also be a change for children. If children have attended childcare in NSW, most often lunch will have been provided. It would usually have consisted of a cooked meal, prepared by a person with background and training in nutrition for young children. The timing of lunch in childcare is usually around midday, so that there is time for children to have a rest after lunch. Schools provide neither the cooked meal nor the rest period. Children may have to wait until well after midday for lunch and have fewer opportunities to snack before this (usually a short recess occurs at about 11 a.m.).

The importance of meals and eating, as well as toileting, lies in the expectations of children's self-regulation. One of the major areas of development for young children relates to their developing ability to recognize states and to self-regulate (Shonkoff and Phillips 2000). One of the major changes in expectations as children start school is being expected to fit a regulatory pattern of visiting the toilet at specific times and eating at specific times.

Other aspects of duty of care relate to the arrival and departure of children. In prior-to-school settings, parents sign children in, leave them with a carer and can be assured that someone knows their child has arrived. At school, children arrive largely unbeknownst to teachers. While supervision arrangements are usually in place to guide the Kindergarten children to their parents/carers at the end of the school day, this is not necessarily the case for all children at school. Teachers in some schools supervise children catching buses, despite some union recommendations to the contrary, but otherwise children take responsibility for getting themselves home, to waiting parents or to other after school arrangements.

Children at school are charged with the responsibility of taking care of themselves in many ways. Hygiene, for example, is the responsibility of individuals. It often involves some unfamiliar environments, such as school toilets and bubblers (drinking fountains). The physical set up of the different environments is noticeable, with school toilets offering much more privacy, but less potential for assistance, than toilets in prior-to-school settings. Children are sometimes anxious about making sure they enter the right toilets—boys or girls—and some boys are unfamiliar with urinals. They are also anxious about being seen to make mistakes in such important places.

Communication between home and school

One of the most consistent comments from families about the move to school involves the marked change in communication between settings and home (Dockett and Perry 2004b). Peters (2000) reports the same issue, whereby children starting school assume a pivotal role in communication between parents and the school. Notes are distributed at school and sent home with children. Generally in schools, there are fewer opportunities for one-to-one interaction between parent and teacher. There is an expectation that children will assume much of the responsibility for transmitting information about what is happening at school and what is required of parents.

Approaches to discipline

After only a few days at school, children start to use the language of school discipline policies. Comments such as 'I got a house point for that', or 'you get a chance card for doing good things' indicate a growing awareness of the often explicit extrinsic award and reward system operating at school.

Most NSW schools have a school-wide discipline policy, based on rewards for positive behaviour and demerits of some sort for negative behaviour. It is not long before children talk about the 'time out chair', 'detention', 'withdrawal' and the difference between these. In one Kindergarten class the shock of 'getting your name on the board' and then not knowing how to get it off, caused considerable anxiety for a group of new school children.

This extensive extrinsic system contrasts with approaches to self-regulation or guidance, rather than discipline, in many prior-to-school settings. Certainly, many prior-to-school settings use extrinsic rewards such as stickers and stamps. The difference is that in schools, there is an extensive and intricate system of rewards. For example, in one school, five class awards entitles the child to a 'principal's patch' they can wear on their uniform. Five principal's patches get the child a bronze award and so on. In her introduction to parents, the Kindergarten (first year of school) teacher in this school indicated that it was very rare for children to attain five class awards in one year; it would more likely take children until the second year of school to attain the next level of award, and some children would never attain this. For young children, such long-term rewards may seem almost unachievable.

The focus on rewards and awards has a number of implications for children, particularly relating to self-perception and identity. A conversation with one Kindergarten child in this class included the following description of himself and his fellow students:

> *Walter is good and smart.*
> *I'm bad and smart.*
> *Michael is just bad.*

A child who regularly sees their name listed on the board as having transgressed may well come to believe that they are just a 'naughty' or 'bad' person, as did the child who made the comments above. It is not suggested that similar experiences do not happen in prior-to-school settings. Rather, these settings with their less intricate reward systems may well offer greater opportunities for children to redeem themselves.

Safety

There are many situations in and around school that vary considerably from situations children will have managed in prior-to-school and home settings. Playgrounds differ, with school playgrounds typically having less equipment available and many more children in any one area.

Parents often mention playground supervision as an issue of concern. In contrast to playgrounds in prior-to-school settings, which are well-fenced, have multiple fixed and loose equipment, and maintain staff:child ratios of no more than 1:8, school playgrounds are often unfenced, cover large expanses of grass or asphalt, have limited equipment and significantly higher ratios of children to staff.

In one school, children were excited to find that they could play on 'the rock', a large outcrop of granite approximately 3 m high, located in the school playground. While on, the one hand, pleased that children had a playground with some interesting natural features, parents also expressed some concern that the rock and the hard ground surrounding it represented a major change from the safety conscious playgrounds of prior-to-school settings.

Children are expected to operate within the outdoor environment, complete with 'big kids' and competing games such as soccer or cricket. Parents note that children starting school often come home with skinned knees or grazes. One parent commenting on her son's experiences noted:

> When he got home and I asked him what he wanted for dinner, he just lost it. He cried and cried and cried. He had hurt his knee quite badly and it was sore. It was like he had contained all his emotion at school and when he got home it just burst out. At childcare or at home, he probably would have had someone cuddle him, help him clean it up and maybe just check how he was. At school, he went to the sick bay and got a band aid and he was keen to go back and play, but it's like he had to hold all his feelings in, just to get through the rest of the day.

In addition to the physical safety of the playground in this instance, there are clear links to the social changes children encounter, as they are expected to become more self-reliant, and less dependent on others for support.

A further area of difference between schools and home or prior-to-school settings related to road safety. One of the consequences of feeling 'big' as they go to school can be that children and adults over-estimate the children's capabilities in areas such as road safety. School children are not as keen as younger children to be seen holding an adult's hand as they cross the road, or negotiate cars and traffic around the school area. Sometimes it is expected that young children will competently catch a bus to and from school, ride their bike or walk themselves to and from school.

Discussion

When children start school they enter an educational environment that is quite different from other environments they have experienced. Quite quickly, they are expected to adapt to the changing demands of school, both in terms of curriculum and the nature of the environment.

Children's images of themselves as learners change as they start school, and adult perceptions of children change as well. One major area of change relates to the expectations held of children. Teachers in schools and parents expect children to assume greater responsibility for caring for themselves and their possessions, eating appropriately, personal hygiene, communication between school and families, and in managing their own safety. The aim of this chapter is to ask how appropriate these changed expectations are and to consider the implications of these changed expectations. For example, are young children in a position to make appropriate judgements about safety? Is it reasonable to expect children to be responsible for communication between home and school?

Most children look forward to school. They enjoy being at school and are well aware that school is a different place from prior-to-school settings. In their words, 'school is a BIG place'. How can we ensure that our expectations of children are not just as overwhelming?

The aim of this chapter is not to position children as victims—neither as victims of school nor as victims of their own inability to manage change. Rather, the aim is to prompt the adults involved in transition to consider the magnitude of change children are expected to manage and to reflect on what can be done to assist children. The breadth of change experienced by children and the ease with which many of them respond to this change, is remarkable. If anything, it should serve as a reminder to adults of the competence of young children as they negotiate an environment different from others they have experienced in terms of philosophy, social and physical demands.

A further aim of this chapter is to ask whether it is reasonable for the adults involved in the transition to school to expect that it will be the children who will make the majority of changes. There are many ways in which adults can assist children as they start school. Children all have different experiences, expectations and perceptions as they start school. Responding positively to these differences requires the adults involved in transition to get to know individual children.

While the majority of children make the transition to school with apparent ease (Cox 1999), many others experience difficulties (Rimm-Kaufman et al. 2000). In turn, many of these difficulties are contextually based and not things over which children have control. For example, Germino-Hausken and Rathburn (2002) describe not only child factors, but also family and school factors as having an impact on children's adjustment to school.

Transition to school is about building up solid, meaningful and long-lasting relationships among all of the participants (Dockett and Perry 2001; Dunlop and Fabian 2003; Pianta and Cox 1999; Rimm-Kaufman and Pianta 2000). This cannot be done if the expectation of the most experienced participants—the adults—is that the least experienced participants—the children—will make the great bulk of the change necessary to ensure a successful start to school. While the children need to be supported in the changes they are expected to make, they also need to see that the important adults around them are also changing. Children need our respect and our recognition of the ways in which they manage change, as well as some leeway when that change can become just too much.

References

Board of Studies, NSW (2000) *The Primary Curriculum 2000: An Overview*. Available at: http://www.bosnsw-k6.nsw.edu.au/parents/pdf_doc/prim_curr00.pdf (accessed 9 February 2005).

Cox, M. (1999) Making the transition, *Early Developments*, 3(1): 4–6.

Dockett, S. and Perry, B. (1999a) Starting school: what do the children say? *Early Child Development and Care*, 159: 107–19.

Dockett, S. and Perry, B. (1999b) *Starting School: What Matters for Children, Parents and Educators*. Canberra: Australian Early Childhood Association.

Dockett, S. and Perry, B. (eds) (2001) *Beginning School Together: Sharing Strengths*. Canberra: Australian Early Childhood Association.

Dockett, S. and Perry, B. (2002) Beliefs and expectations of parents, prior-to-school educators and school teachers as children start school. *Australian Association for Research in Education Refereed Conference Proceedings*. Available at: www.aare.edu.au (accessed 9 February 2005).

Dockett, S. and Perry, B. (2004a) 'School is like preschool but you can't make noise': young children's views of continuity from preschool (nursery) to school, *OMEP Updates*, No. 116: 16–20.

Dockett, S. and Perry, B. (2004b) Starting school: perspectives of Australian children, parents and educators, *Journal of Early Childhood Research*, 2(2): 171–89.

Dockett, S., Perry, B. and Nicolson, D. (2002) Social and personal transformation as children start school, *International Journal of Learning*, 19: 289–99.

Dunlop, A-W. (2004) Do differences in early education environments make a difference to children's curricular experience on transition to school? Poster Symposium, *Transitions in Early Education: Are There Curricular Implications?*

EECERA 2004 14th Annual Conference of the European Early Childhood Education Research Association, 1–4 September, Malta.

Dunlop, A-W. and Fabian, H. (2003) Editorial, *Transitions. European Early Childhood Education*, Research Monograph Series No. 1: 2–4.

Fabian, H. (2002) *Children Starting School.* London: Fulton.

Germino-Hausken, E. and Rathbun, A. (2002, April) Adjustment to kindergarten: Child, family and Kindergarten program factors. Paper presented at the annual meeting of the American Educational Research Association, New Orleans.

McGough, R. (n.d.) First day at school. Available at: http://www.poemhunter.com/p/m/poem.asp?poet=6667andpoem=31105 (accessed 9 February 2005).

Meredith, M., Perry, B., Dockett, S. and Borg, T. (1999) Changes in parents' perceptions of their children's transition to school: first child and later children, *Journal of Australian Research in Early Childhood Education*, 6(2): 228–39.

New South Wales Department of Community Services (2002) *New South Wales curriculum framework for children's services: The practice of relationships, essential provisions for children's services.* Sydney: NSW DoCS.

Perry, B., Dockett, S. and Howard, P. (2000) Starting school: issues for children, parents and teachers, *Journal of Australian Research in Early Childhood Education*, 7(1): 41–53.

Peters, S. (2000, August) Multiple perspectives on continuity in early learning and the transition to school. Paper presented at the Early Childhood Education Research Association Conference, London. ED 447916.

Pianta, R. (2004) Going to Kindergarten: transition models and practices. Proceedings of the International Conference, Continuity and change: transitions in education (CD Rom), Sydney, 27–28 November.

Pianta, R.C. and Cox, M.E. (1999) *The Transition to Kindergarten.* Baltimore, MD: Paul H. Brookes Publishing.

Rimm-Kaufman, S.E. and Pianta, R.C. (2000) An ecological perspective on the transition to kindergarten: a theoretical framework to guide empirical research, *Journal of Applied Developmental Psychology*, 21(5): 491–511.

Rimm-Kaufman, S.E., Pianta, R.C. and Cox, M.J. (2000) Teachers' judgements of problems in the transition to kindergarten, *Early Childhood Research Quarterly*, 15: 147–66.

Shonkoff, J. and Phillips, D. (eds) (2000) *From Neurons to Neighbourhoods: The Science of Early Childhood Development.* Washington, DC: National Academy Press.

PARENTS AND PROFESSIONALS SUPPORTING TRANSITIONS

A common theme running throughout this section is the notion of partnership. The first chapter sets the scene by exploring the way in which practitioners can support children's transition to school through understanding individual's backgrounds, and taking into account characteristics, skills, abilities and experiences. The interplay between their personal characteristics, relationships and experiences, and the way they vary in their susceptibility to the effects of major social change is highlighted. The implication is that a personalized learning and transition system is needed, including the early identification of children at risk of adjusting and coping with school.

There is increased recognition of the importance of working collaboratively with parents in the transition to school. In Singapore these initiatives have been sponsored by government organizations, as well as private and welfare organizations. The second chapter in this section outlines a parent empowerment programme in which a combination of parent workshops, and parent- and child-guided play sessions were conducted during the last 6 months in preschool. Orientation meetings prior to school entry can improve ongoing two-way home–school communications, as can parent workshops, teacher–parent conferences and family social events.

In England, as in several other countries, children encounter two contrasting curricula either side of the transition to school, which are based on two very different views of how children learn. In preschool services, learning is largely through the medium of play and is based on the premise that parents and practitioners collaborate to promote learning. However, the school curriculum is divided into subject knowledge and emphasizes observable, testable outcomes with opportunities to learn through play becoming less frequent. The transition to school is therefore much more complex than a physical move or one that entails forming new relationships. The change in curriculum poses challenges for all participants and the final chapter in this section explores the perceptions of this transition, and considers how the expectations of teachers, children and parents might be affected by the change in curriculum and considers the implications this might have for children's learning.

8 Understanding and supporting children: shaping transition practices

Kay Margetts

Understanding the variation in children's development, and personal, family and background experiences that impact on children's adjustment to school is critical for developing policies and practices related to early schooling (Rimm-Kauffman et al. 2000), and in particular, the transition to school.

This transition is complex, and involves the adjustment to a range of new experiences and physical, social/behavioural, and academic challenges and expectations. The way in which each child responds has the potential to impact on their progress and future schooling. For some children the adjustment to the new setting, and the ability to make meaning and understand what is expected of them is relatively straightforward, for other children it is more difficult. It has been suggested that risk factors in the early years of schooling increase children's vulnerability for difficulties in the next 10–12 years and may persist into later life (Belsky and MacKinnon 1994; Cowan et al. 1994; Kienig 2000; Taylor 1998).

The ecological model of child development provides a comprehensive framework for understanding this complexity. In this model, the variability in children's development and adjustment to school is influenced by a number of interdependent factors including biological and developmental characteristics, and social and cultural factors. At the level of the microsystem, development is influenced by the interactions of the child's personal characteristics with the settings that form the basis of their daily life— home, family, preschool, school and local community. The next level or exosystem, indirectly influences children's development and includes parental employment, socio-economic status, and a range of government policies and practices. More broadly, the components of the macrosystem shape children's development through the subculture or dominant beliefs and ideologies of the society in which the child lives (Bronfenbrenner 1979, 1986). However, it is the combination of the child's personal characteristics, their experiences, and the interconnections between home, preschool and school that ultimately determines how a child adjusts to school (Margetts 2002).

Personal challenges

Children have different responses to starting school and vary in their susceptibility to the effects of major social experiences (Rutter and Rutter 1992). The immense variety in their development and experiences makes each child's transition to school unique. Most children commence the first year of formal schooling at around 5 or 6 years of age when they are typically in the process of important development in a variety of areas including:

- self-awareness;
- emotional understanding;
- moral judgements;
- peer relationships;
- forming simple symbolic concepts;
- mastering increasingly complex physical skills;
- independent self-help skills (Love and Yelton 1989).

These developments and changes are of themselves challenging to the child, and are often compounded by the tensions and uncertainties associated with starting school as children take on a new identity or role, and the behaviours and demands associated with being a school child (Entwisle et al. 1987; Griebel and Niesel 2000). The range of physical, social and academic challenges in the new setting often are more easily met when children can (Ledger et al. 1998) function independently, develop relationships with staff and peers, conform to rules, and behave in ways that are appropriate for the class and school. Early difficulties have the potential to impact on children's academic and personal development. The passage through this major social change is so critical that Dunlop (2000) has suggested that it may have a lasting influence on how children view themselves, how others value them, their sense of wellbeing and their ability to learn. When children commence schooling neuro-developmentally and behaviourally immature, and with poor self-regulation and attentional capacities, they often fall behind the rest of the class. Behavioural problems may arise as a reaction to difficulties in coping with learning and academic demands, and the new environment, which then generate anger, frustration, despair and insecurity (Prior 1996).

Understanding adjustment

Adjustment to school involves two types of skills: conventional academic skills, and social/behavioural skills. Children benefit when they have a positive self-image about academic learning, social functioning, and the ability to cope with the challenges of school (Belsky and MacKinnon 1994). Academic skills include classroom orientation and involvement, work habits, intelligent behaviour, and understandings about literacy and numeracy (Ladd et al. 1997; Harrison and Ungerer 2000; Margetts 2003a). Low levels of academic skills and social behavioural difficulties at school appear to be related (Merrell and Tymms 2001).

Social skills that support adjustment include social competence, problem-solving skills, self-reliance and determinations, cooperative behaviours, non-disruptive group entry strategies and skilled verbal communication skills (Fabian 2000a; Maxwell and Eller 1994). Many of these skills and understandings are inter-related. Difficulties are likely to arise when children are:

- non-compliant, such as when they are resistant to following directions;
- disorganized, such as when they can't organize their equipment, work space or work time;
- distractible, such as when they are overcome by what is going on around them;
- anti-social and have difficulty considering the rights of others.

(Margetts, 2002)

The level of comfort, familiarity and predictability children experience may also influence this adjustment. 'For young children, the transition ... to schooling is the intersection of different cultures' (Clancy et al. 2001: 56) in which children are required to make and share meaning. To this extent, knowing about 'not knowing' and what to do about it (Fabian 2000b) and 'knowing the rules' is important (Dockett et al. 1997). Children are at risk of not adjusting easily to school when there is a mismatch between the skills, attitudes and knowledge they bring to school, and the expectations and culture of the school itself (Clancy et al. 2001).

Influences on children's development and adjustment

Children's development and adjustment are impacted by their personal characteristics and cultural background, including family structure, economic status and experiences. Research suggests that gender, temperament, ordinal position in the family (Bates et al. 1994), self-awareness (Love and Yelton 1989), self-esteem (Verschueren et al. 1996), self-regulatory behaviours (Michels et al. 1993), and peer relationships or acceptance (Ladd and Price 1989; Maxwell and Eller 1994) are important.

Boys generally have more difficulty than girls adjusting to school. They are more likely to have lower levels of social skills (Spitzer et al. 1995; National Institute of Child Health and Human Development (NICHD) Early Child Care Research Network 2001) including cooperation and self-control (Margetts 2003), and social understanding (Porath 2003), and higher levels of general maladjustment, aggressiveness including conflict with adults, externalizing behaviour, internalizing behaviour and hyperactivity (Spitzer et al. 1995; Margetts 2003; NICHD, 2003). Boys rated as insecure or avoidant have also shown inhibited levels of social participation (Moss et al. 1998).

Age appears to be barely significant in relation to school adjustment (Spitzer et al. 1995; Margetts, 2003). In an Australian study by Margetts (2003), children who were relatively older than their class mates when they commenced school were rated by teachers as slightly more academically competent in the first year of school. However, age did not contribute significantly to children's social skills or behaviour.

The way that children cope with stress and school adjustment may vary in relation to temperamental characteristics, as well as with the features, demands and values of the school setting (Rothbart and Bates, 1998). Anxiety associated with starting school can manifest itself in children's social and behavioural responses (Fabian 2000b). Children who are shy, withdrawn or cautious about new situations, resistant to direction, show frequent negative emotional responses or are reactive, are more likely to have difficulty adjusting to school than other children (Rothbart and Bates 1998).

Social skills and relationships are important. Cooperation, assertion and self-control, including following teachers directions, producing correct school work, ignoring peer distractions, group entry strategies, initiating conversations with peers, responding appropriately to peer pressure, controlling oneself in conflict situations, have been strongly associated with children's adjustment to school. These skills have been significantly associated with low levels of behaviour problems and high levels of academic competence (Margetts 2004). Furthermore, children's social understanding, including how well they understand their own role and their ability to interpret the feeling and intentions of others, contributes to adjustment (Porath 2003).

A strong link has been suggested between peer acceptance, friendship and satisfying relationships with a few peers, and better school adjustment. Children had significantly higher levels of social skills and academic competence, and less problem behaviours when they commenced school with a familiar playmate in the same class (Margetts 1997). They were more likely to be cooperative and non-aggressive (Belsky and MacKinnon 1994), to have favourable attitudes toward school and exhibit less anxiety. Children who established new friendships within the first 2 months of schooling showed more positive gains in school performance (Maxwell and Eller 1994; Ladd et al. 1997; Fabian 2000a). Interestingly, children who associated with younger peers at preschool were more likely to have negative attitudes toward school than children who had associated with same age or older peers (Ladd and Price 1987).

Whether or not children have older siblings appears to influence their adjustment to school. In an Australian study, first-born children tended to have lower levels of cooperation, and higher levels of externalizing behaviour, than subsequent or younger children in a family (Margetts 2003a). This may be because children with older siblings, and their parents, are more likely to have knowledge and understanding of the school culture, including academic skills, and the children are more likely to be exposed to, and imitate behaviours associated with cooperation, self-regulation and responding appropriately to frustration.

Family background and experiences

Within the ecological model, sociocultural contexts are powerful influences on children's development and transition to school. Race, ethnicity, language spoken at home, and socio-economic status influence children's developmental processes and competencies. In some families, the parents of children have little understanding or experience of the school culture into which they and their child are entering (Clancy et al. 2001).

When children can understand and use the language of their peers and teachers, and relate to the ideas and topics of classroom activities, they are more likely to feel competent in school. Schooling in Australia occurs within an English speaking context, and children who do not speak English at home are at increased risk of dislocation when placed in school environments where English is the language of instruction. Studies in Australia have shown that children who spoke English at home had better social skills, fewer problem behaviours and higher levels of academic competence (Margetts 1994), compliance, language skills and communication (Ochiltree and Edgar 1995) than children who did not speak English at home.

More positive school adjustment has been associated with children from households with comparatively greater economic resources. High socio-economic status is a significant contributor to lower levels of externalizing/ aggressive behaviour and adult/child conflict in the first year of school (NICHD, 2003). In the Australian study by Margetts (2003a), children from families with relatively higher levels of income were more likely to have:

- better adjustment, including higher levels of cooperation, assertion and overall social skills;
- lower levels of internalizing behaviour and overall problem behaviour;
- higher levels of academic competence.

In addition, parent level of employment in the year children commenced schooling impacted on their social, behavioural and academic adjustment. Having parents in full-time employment contributed positively to children's adjustment to school. It may be, as suggested by Taylor (1998), that full-time employment brings stability to a child's life, and the orderliness associated with full-time employment benefits children as they face the uncertainties and possible dislocations associated with the transition to schooling.

Children's experiences

Increasing numbers of children experience different types of parental and non-parental child care for varying hours, and there is concern about the influence of this care on children's development and their progress in school. While a number of reports have shown positive developmental outcomes related to extensive non-maternal child care (Andersson 1989; Broberg et al. 1989), more recent ecologically-based studies have raised some concerns. Belsky (2001) concluded that more extensive, continuous non-maternal child care was predictive of lower levels of socio-emotional development. The American NICHD study (2003) reported that children who spent more time in non-maternal care between birth and 56 months of age, had higher levels of externalizing/aggressive behaviour and adult/child conflict in the first year of school than other children.

In Australian studies, associations have been identified between children who received an average of 20 hours or more of child care per week across the years prior to school, and more non-compliance at school (Ochiltree and Edgar 1995). In the study by Margetts (2003b), children who attended centre-based child care for 4 or 5 days per week, or more than 30 hours per week were at risk of lower levels of social skills and academic competence, and more problem behaviours as they started school. The results were particularly strong in relation to the extent of care in the 2 years closer to birth and developmental outcomes. By contrast, attendance at preschool (with tertiary qualified staff and typically for 10–12 hours per week) predicted benefits for children as they commenced school. Children who attended 3-year-old pre-school had higher levels of cooperation and lower levels of externalizing behaviour. Attendance at 4-year-old preschool in the year prior to schooling, predicted higher levels of cooperation, self-control and academic compe-tence. More hours per week of 4-year-old preschool predicted lower levels of problem behaviour.

The influence of transition to school programmes

The '. . . degree of difficulty in negotiating the transition to school is closely related to how well the school culture is understood in the home environment, and the degree of trust and respect implicit in this understanding' (Clancy et al. 2001: 60). There are many children and families who have little knowledge or understanding of particular school cultures including the implicit rules, organization and structures (Clancy et al. 2001). Adjustment is supported when children and their families participate in comprehensive prior-to-school transition programmes that are designed to familiarize participants with the school environment, and the challenges and demands associated with starting school (Margetts 1997; Broström 2000). For example, when children and their families participated in six or more transition activities, children had higher levels of assertion, self-control, overall social skills, and academic competence (Margetts 2003a). Opportunities to visit and participate in the school, assist children (and their families) to construct their own realities and meanings and adapt to the culture of the school (Fabian 2000b), and schools gain valuable understandings of children and their families.

Teacher interactions also contribute to children's adjustment. When teachers made an effort to engage in social interactions in the first year of school with children who were anxious, internalizing and reticent to engage in social interactions, there was evidence of good adjustment at the start of the following school year (Pianta and Nimetz 1991). Similarly, Fabian (2000b) reported student wellbeing and adjustment to school were supported when teachers encouraged less communicatively competent children to express themselves more effectively, and carefully organized and structured the social setting so that social relations were supported and expectations clearly expressed. When teachers have demonstrated developmentally inappropriate instructional practices children exhibited more stress behaviours than children in classes where teachers used more developmentally appropriate practices (Burts et al. 1990, cited in Maxwell and Eller 1994).

This overview of children's development and adjustment to school contributes to understandings about transition to school, and leads to a number of implications or principles for practice. While much of the research has been conducted in western nations, it is likely that these principles could have broader relevance.

Implications for practice

Given the complexity of school adjustment, and the wide range of skills, knowledge and experiences that children bring with them to school, *transition programmes need to be based on a sound understanding of children, families and communities.* This information can be gained when transition programmes create links between, and actively involve children, parents, families, teachers, early childhood services, schools and the local community. When a partnership approach is adopted and the 'voice' of all participants is valued, the sharing of important information is facilitated. This should lead to the development of relevant support mechanisms that assist children and their families in the transition between home, preschool and school, and minimize changes and discontinuities.

The kinds of experiences that children encounter as they make sense of relatively new surroundings, routines and procedures, and learn what behaviour is considered appropriate may have far reaching effects on their social and academic success. *Transition programmes should value and support continuity of children's development and learning, prior-to-school experiences, relationships and social expectations, and encourage children's independence and successful functioning.* Teachers should reflect on the extent to which practices in the early weeks of schooling are familiar to children and responsive to the diversity of their backgrounds, needs and abilities. In response, programmes and practices should be flexible, inclusive, and responsive to the local community and its complexity, and demonstrate respect for and acceptance of diversity, and the needs of all involved.

Understanding and experience of the school setting, including its organization, rules and structures is an important part of transition. *Children and their families should be given many opportunities, both formal and informal, to visit the school prior to commencement.* This gives them opportunities to make sense of the new sociocultural contexts, and to make and share meaning, including the establishment of new relationships and friendships. Schools can also gain valuable understandings about new entrants and their families.

Schools should be encouraged to provide additional or targeted opportunities for children who are at risk of adjustment difficulties.

- those with developmental difficulties;
- from low socio-economic backgrounds;
- who do not speak the language of instruction at home;
- children who do not attend preschool;
- those from diverse cultural groups.

As noted previously, social and academic outcomes in the preschool years are predictive of children's adjustment to the first year of schooling, and problem behaviours in the early years, including extreme overactivity, inability to sit still, short attention span, emotional difficulties and negative attitude predict behaviour problems in adolescence. It is important that these children are identified as early as possible and preferably prior to the commencement of school.

Encouragement should be provided for the development of culturally important academic and social understanding and skills, prior to school. For example, in Western nations, strategies should help children develop confidence in their own abilities, take responsibility for their own actions and behaviours, and develop particular academic skills and conceptual knowledge. Children should have an awareness of letters and numbers, they should be able to handle a book and to turn pages. They should be able to concentrate and complete simple tasks. Children should be encouraged to have conversations with other children and adults, and to talk about their own experiences and ideas, and ask for help from adults. It is important that this occurs in ways that do not denigrate the values and practices of other cultures.

Given the importance of social skills for children's wellbeing and adjustment, they should be supported to interact with peers and adults in positive ways, and in conflict and non-conflict situations. This includes encouragement to listen to others, share, take turns, cooperate and follow reasonable instructions. When children are given consistent guidance and support in being responsible for controlling their feelings, and behaving in acceptable ways without disturbing or hurting others, they are more likely to exhibit self-control. This is further supported when they are encouraged to take responsibility for their actions and their belongings, and to follow reasonable rules and expectations. They can be encouraged to persevere with difficult tasks such as completing a puzzle, working out how to prevent a block tower from collapsing, or practising hitting a target with a ball. Independence and self-reliance are also fostered when children master a range of physical skills such as managing their own clothing, toileting, nose blowing and feeding; and can coordinate their bodies to run, jump, climb, throw and catch, to control a pencil, and cut with scissors.

At preschool, strategies can include staff delaying and decreasing their attention and praise, reducing instructions and prompts, assigning roles and responsibilities, including school uniforms and bags in dramatic play areas, and photographs of school experiences in the book area or on display boards. It is important that preschool staff are familiar with school practices so that they can accurately respond to children's questions and establish realistic expectations. However, it is important to heed the warning by Bredekamp and Copple (1997) that a developmentally appropriate early childhood programme should not be changed to be more like an inappropriate school class.

The importance of friendships and familiar relationships should be recognized in allocating children to classes such as pairing children with friends and placing children from the same preschool or child care centre in the same class, and in encouraging the development of friendships for children who may commence school without a familiar playmate.

Creating and sustaining effective transition programmes is a multifaceted challenge that should involve governments, schools, families and local communities. There is widespread agreement that programmes should be based on a philosophy that children's adjustment to school is easier when children are familiar with the new situation, parents are informed about the new school, and teachers have information about children's development and previous experiences, and school experiences can be adapted to minimize changes and discontinuities. The goal that children should experience a smooth, coherent and comprehensive transition appears to be largely unmet or left to chance in most countries. Despite compelling evidence for the benefits of early identification and support for children and families at risk of poor developmental trajectories, and the critical importance of early school adjustment, transition to school receives little, or no official support at the policy or fiscal levels. This may be because research about transitions and their impact on children is in its infancy, and more information is needed not only about the efficacy of particular approaches, for particular cohorts of the population, but also the long-term social, emotional and academic benefits of these approaches. We must also consider the extent to which transition principles and practices are applicable within and across different racial or ethnic groups also needs to be identified. What is clear, is that a stronger voice is needed for our young children and their families as they make the transition to school.

References

Andersson, B. (1989) Effects of public day-care: a longitudinal study, *Child Development*, 60: 857–66.

Bates, J., Marvinney, D., Kelly, T., Dodge, K., Bennett, D. & Pettit, G. (1994). Childcare history and kindergarten adjustment. *Developmental Psychology*, 30(5), 690–700.

Belsky, J. (2001) Developmental risks (still) associated with early child care, *Journal of Child Psychology and Psychiatry*, 42: 845–60.

Belsky, J. and MacKinnon, C. (1994) Transition to school: Developmental trajectories and school experiences, *Early Education and Development*, 5(2): 106–19.

Bredekamp, S. and Copple, C. (eds) (1997) *Developmentally Appropriate Practice in Early Childhood Programmes*. Washington, DC: National Association for the Education of Young Children.

Broberg, A., Hwang, C., Lamb, M. and Ketterlinus, R. (1989) Child care effects on socioemotional and intellectual competence in Swedish preschoolers, in J. S. Lande, S. Scarr and N. Gunzenhauser (eds) *Caring for Children: Challenge to America*. Hillsdale: Lawrence Erlbaum Associates.

Bronfenbrenner, U. (1979) *The Ecology of Human Development: Experiments by Nature and Design*. Cambridge, MA: Harvard University Press.

Bronfenbrenner, U. (1986) Ecology of the family as a context for human development: research perspectives, *Developmental Psychology*, 22: 723–33.

Broström, S. (2000) Transition to school. Paper presented at the EECERA 10th European Conference on Quality in Early Childhood Education, London, August 29–September 1, 2000.

Clancy, S., Simpson, L. and Howard, P. (2001) Mutual trust and respect, in S. Dockett and B. Perry (eds) *Beginning School Together: Sharing Strengths*. Watson: Australian Early Childhood Association Inc.

Cowan, P., Cowan, C., Shulz, M. and Henning, G. (1994) Prebirth to preschool family factors in children's adaptation to kindergarten, in R. Parke and S. Kellart (eds) *Exploring Family Relationships with Other Social Contexts*. Hillsdale, NJ: Lawrence Erlbaum Associates.

Dockett, S., Perry, R. and Tracey, D. (1997) Getting ready for school. Paper presented at the Australian Association for Research in Education Annual Conference, Brisbane, December, 1–4 1997.

Dunlop, A-W. (2000) Perspectives on the child as a learner: Should educators' views of preschool and primary children differ? Paper presented at the EECERA 10th European Conference on Quality in Early Childhood Education, London, August 29–September 1, 2000.

Entwisle, D., Alexander, K., Cadigan, D. and Pallas, A. (1987) The emergent academic self image of first graders, *Child Development*, 58: 1190–206.

Fabian, H. (2000a) Empowering children for transitions. Paper presented at the EECERA 10th European Conference on Quality in Early Childhood Education, London, August 29–September 1, 2000.

Fabian, H. (2000b) Small steps to starting school, *International Journal of Early Years Education*, 8(2): 141–53.

Griebel, W. and Niesel, R. (2000) The children's voice in the complex transition into kindergarten and school. Paper presented at the EECERA 10th European Conference on Quality in Early Childhood Education, London, August 29–September 1, 2000.

Harrison, L. and Ungerer, J. (2000) Children and child care: a longitudinal study of the relationships between developmental outcomes and use of nonparental care from birth to six. Paper prepared for the Department of Family and Community Services, Panel Data and Policy Conference, Canberra, May, 2000.

Kienig, A. (2000) Transitions in early childhood. Paper presented at the EECERA 10th European Conference on Quality in Early Childhood Education, London, August 29–September 1, 2000.

Ladd, G., Kochenderfer, B. & Coleman, C. (1997). Classroom peer acceptance, friendship, and victimization: Distinct relational systems that contribute uniquely to Children's School Adjustment? *Child Development*, 68(6), 1181–1197.

Ladd, J. and Price, J. (1987) Predicting children's social and school adjustment following the transition from preschool to kindergarten, *Child Development*, 58(5): 1168–89.

Ledger, E., Smith, A. and Rich, P. (1998) 'Do I go to school to get a brain?' The transition from kindergarten to school from the child's perspective, *Childrenz Issues*, 2(1): 7–11.

Love, J.M. and Yelton, B. (1989) Smoothing the road from preschool to kindergarten, *Principal*, 68(5): 26–7.

Margetts, K. (1994). *Children's adjustment to the first year of schooling*. Unpublished Master of Education Thesis, The University of Melbourne. Melbourne.

Margetts, (1997) Factors impacting on children's adjustment to the first year of primary school. *set: Research Information for Teachers*, 2: 1–4.

Margetts, K. (2002) Planning transition programmes, in H. Fabian and W-A. Dunlop (eds) *Transitions in the Early Years*. London: RoutledgeFalmer.

Margetts, K. (2003a) Children bring more to school than their backpacks: Starting school downunder, *European Early Childhood Education Research Monograph: Transitions*, 1: 5–14.

Margetts, K. (2003b) Relationships between centre-based child care and children's adjustment to the first year of school. Paper presented at the 13th European Conference on Quality in Early Childhood Education: Early Childhood Narratives, Glasgow, Scotland, 3–6 September 2003.

Margetts, K. (2004) Identifying and supporting behaviours associated with co-operation, assertion and self-control in young children starting school, *European Early Childhood Education Research Journal*, 12(2): 75–86.

Maxwell, K. and Eller, S., (1994) Children's transition to kindergarten, *Young Children*, 49(6): 56–63.

Merrell, C. and Tymms, P. (2001) Inattention, hyperactivity and impulsiveness: their impact on academic achievement and progress, *British Journal of Educational Psychology*, 71: 43–56.

Michels, S., Pianta, R. and Reeve, R. (1993) Parent self-reports of discipline practices and child acting-out behaviors in kindergarten, *Early Education and Development*, 4(2): 139–44.

Moss, E., Rousseau, D., Parent, S., St-Laurent, D. and Saintonge, J. (1998) Correlates of attachment at school age: maternal reported stress, mother-child interaction, and behaviour problems, *Child Development*, 69(5): 1390–405.

National Institute of Child Health and Human Development (NICHD) Early Child Care Research Network (2001) Early child care and children's development prior to school entry. Paper presented at the Society for Research in Child Development Biennial Meeting. Minneapolis, April, 20–23 2001.

National Institute of Child Health and Human Development (NICHD) Early Child Care Research Network (2003). Does amount of time spent in child care predict socioemotional adjustment during the transition to kindergarten? *Child Development*. 74(4) 976–1005.

Ochiltree, G. and Edgar, D. (1995) Today's child care, tomorrow's children! *AIFS*

Early Childhood Study Paper No. 7. Melbourne: Australian Institute of Family Studies.

Pianta, R. and Nimetz, S. (1991) Relationships between children and teachers: Associations with home and classroom behavior, *Journal of Applied Developmental Psychology*, 12: 379–93.

Porath, M. (2003) Social understanding in the first years of school, *Early Childhood Research Quarterly*, 18: 468–84.

Prior, M. (1996) *Learning and Behavioural Difficulties: Implications for Intervention*, Free Public Lecture, University of Melbourne, 30 September, 1996.

Rimm-Kauffman, S., Pianta, R. and Cox, M. (2000) Teachers' judgments of problems in the transition to kindergarten, *Early Childhood Research Quarterly*, 15: 147–66.

Rothbart, M. and Bates, J. (1998) Temperament, in W. Damon and N. Eisenberg (eds) *Handbook of Child Psychology: Social, Emotional, and Personality Development*, vol. 3, 5th edn. New York: Wiley.

Rutter, M. and Rutter, M. (1992) *Developing Minds: Challenges and Continuity Across the Lifespan*. London: Penguin.

Spitzer, S., Cupp, R. and Parke, R. (1995) School entrance age, social acceptance, and self-perceptions in kindergarten and 1st grade, *Early Childhood Research Quarterly*, 10: 433–50.

Taylor, J. (1998) *Life at Six: Life Chances and Beginning School*. Fitzroy: Brotherhood of St Laurence.

Verschueren, K., Marcoen, A. and Schoefs, V. (1996) The internal working model of the self, attachment and competence in five-year-olds, *Child Development*, 67: 2493–511.

9 Parent involvement in the transition to school

Christine Clarke

There has been increased parent involvement in education, especially during the transition phase between preschool and primary school, reported in the international literature during the last 30 years. This has not been the case in many Asian countries including Singapore, although there has been increasing recognition of the importance of working more collaboratively with parents in Singapore preschools and schools since the late 1990s. These initiatives have been sponsored by government organizations, as well as by private and welfare organizations.

This chapter summarizes some of the early childhood research in Singapore and focuses in particular on transition to school studies with a parent involvement component. One particular study, a parent empowerment programme, which was conducted during the last 6 months of preschool, will be described in more detail. It was evaluated by quantitative and qualitative measures during the preschool project with a follow-up during the children's first year in school. The positive findings of this study for both children and parents were disseminated to other preschools and primary schools and several of the practices have subsequently been adopted in other Singapore preschools. The chapter will conclude with recommendations for further initiatives and research into transition to school.

Background

The importance of parent involvement in education has been promoted since the 1970s in the UK and USA (for example, Gordon 1969, 1977; Pugh and De'Ath 1989; Epstein 1995). The essential role that parents could play during the transition from preschool to school has also been emphasized (for example, Cleave et al. 1982; Alexander and Entwistle 1988; Hinton 1989; Parr et al. 1993; Maxwell and Eller 1994; Perry et al. 2000; Raban and Ure 2000; Johansson 2002; Docket and Perry 2004).

In Singapore, researchers have also promoted the benefits of parent involvement particularly in early childhood (Sharpe 1991, 1996; Koo 1993;

Clarke 2000). There has recently been official recognition of the importance of parent involvement in education, for example, COMPASS (Community and Parents in Support of Schools) an initiative established by the Ministry of Education (MOE) in 1998 to increase school, home and community collaboration (MOE 2005).

The research body in Singapore in the area of early childhood education has undergone several shifts in focus. Initially studies focused on child development in the Singapore context (Ko and Ho 1992; Seng and Lazar 1992; Lim 1994; Sharpe 1994, 1997; Tan-Niam 1994), moving next to an examination of quality indicators of preschools (Sharpe 1996; Kwan et al. 1998; Fan-Eng and Sharpe 2000; Kwan 2000, 2001; Retas and Kwan 2000) and, more recently, to new curricula developments in Singapore preschools (Sharpe 2002a; Gan 2004).

There have been fewer studies on the issue of parent involvement in early childhood education in Singapore. Seng (1994) and Sharpe (1991, 1996) examined parental expectations of preschool programmes, while Koo (1993) and Sharpe (1991, 1996) investigated the different roles of parents and teachers in preschool education.

More recently, studies have focused on different aspects of transition to school (Clarke 2000; Clarke and Sharpe 2003; Yeo and Clarke 2005). Of these studies, Clarke (2000) focused primarily on parent involvement during the transition process. This study will be described in more detail in this chapter.

Education in Singapore

Singapore is a small island city-state in South East Asia where education is highly valued by its multiracial populace who are the nation's only natural resource. Since its independence in 1965, the government has pursued a system of meritocracy, which over the years has resulted in a highly competitive, results-driven education system. Parents are anxious for their children's success in school and take great pains to ensure that their goals are achieved (Sharpe 2002a). Although statutory, school attendance only became compulsory in January 2003; the majority of Singaporean children have attended preschool, as well as primary school education since the 1960s. The main medium of instruction in Singapore schools is English, although all children must also study their Mother Tongue (Chinese, Malay and/or Tamil).

Preschool education in Singapore

The government provides financial subsidies for preschool education and care to enable more women to enter the workforce, as well as introducing early education outside the home. Preschool education in Singapore ranges from full day and half-day childcare centres to 2–4-hour kindergarten programmes for children aged 2–6 years. Although preschool education is not mandatory, the majority of children below the age of 7 years attend some kind of preschool facility. Childcare centres and kindergartens are operated by a combination of community foundations, voluntary, welfare and social groups, religious bodies and private businesses.

Responsibility for overseeing preschool centres is divided between two government ministries. The Ministry of Community Development, Youth and Sports (MCYS) have responsibility for promoting and regulating childcare centres, which provide places for children aged 2 months to rising 7-year-olds throughout the year (MCYS 2005). The Ministry of Education (MOE) oversees the provision of kindergartens, which provide half-day educationally orientated programmes for 3–6-year-olds during the academic year. In 2003, the MOE introduced a new curriculum framework including desired outcomes for preschool education in Singapore (Sharpe 2003), which is optional for both kindergartens and childcare centres. The new curriculum guidelines provide more child-centred learning opportunities, is theme-based, and enables children to learn more through play than the earlier primarily subject-based curriculum and teacher-led activities including many paper and pencil activity sheets.

Primary school education in Singapore

Singaporean children start school in January of the year in which they turn 7 years old. The size of primary schools in many Asian countries is much larger than that found in most western countries. Singapore primary schools have an enrolment ranging from 1000 to 2900 pupils between the ages of 6 and 12 years, with nine to twelve classes per year level, and class sizes of 40 pupils. In 2005, the MOE initiated a plan to gradually reduce class sizes, starting with a reduction in Primary One (P1) to no more than 30 pupils per class. Curricula and pedagogical practices in P1 are also currently being revised in line with the more child-centred learning opportunities found in the revised curricula guidelines for kindergartens. Increased liaison between preschools and primary schools is also being encouraged.

Parent involvement in Singapore schools

Ongoing school–home communication varies across schools, but is mainly a one-way communication from school to home through the homework diary, newsletters, and a twice-yearly report book of each child's assessment results and classroom performance. Some schools provide an opportunity for annual parent–teachers conferencing, while others conduct parent-briefing sessions by class or year level. More recently, several schools have introduced parent workshops to explain curricula changes and how different subjects are taught, whilst others have introduced parent volunteering schemes to assist the school with social events, field trips, or as 'reading aunts' to read with children who are slower in reading development. If problems arise teachers or parents may initiate contact by written notes, emails or telephone messages (MOE & COMPASS 2005).

Transition from preschool to school in Singapore

Parents register their children for primary school 5 months prior to school entry. Parents and children are invited to attend an orientation meeting towards the end of the school year or during the school holidays. The briefing is conducted in the school hall by the principal and senior staff for the parents or guardians of the new P1 cohort of 250–400 children. The format for the meeting varies, but generally includes a briefing about the rules and regulations of the school, and basic information about the curricula and assessments. The briefing is usually conducted in English without translations into Mother Tongue (Mandarin, Malay or Tamil) even though English is not the first language of many of the parents. The children meanwhile meet their form teachers and the other children assigned to their class. Making the orientation and transition to school a positive and personalized experience for parents and children can be quite challenging for schools with such large numbers in each new cohort.

It has not been a common practice for kindergartens to visit primary schools with their pupils during the last term before school entry. There are several reasons for this, one being that many primary schools take new entrants from as many as thirty different preschool centres across the island each year and the prospect of so many centres visiting could potentially be both time-consuming and disruptive for the schools. However, under the recent revisions planned for P1, schools are being encouraged to find ways to increase their liaison with their main 'feeder' preschools.

Rationale for increasing parent involvement in education in Asian countries

Traditionally, Singapore parents have seen their main roles in supporting their children's learning and education as ensuring regular school attendance, monitoring homework and funding tuition outside school hours, rather than through direct involvement in their children's schools.

Studies of Chinese parents living in various countries including Mainland China, Taiwan, Hong Kong, Singapore, USA and England have noted the high priority they give to education and to supporting their children's studies at home (for example, Dornbusch et al. 1987; Chen and Stevenson 1989; Sue and Okazaki 1990; Crystal and Stevenson 1991; Steinberg et al. 1991; Sharpe 2002b). However, studies have also generally found low levels of parent involvement in preschool and schools in Taiwan, Hong Kong and Singapore (Sharpe 1991, 1997; Liu and Chien 1998; Lam 1999; Ng 2000). Liu and Chien (1998) suggest that 'this is because many parents feel that they have neither the training, knowledge nor expertise to provide appropriate activities for their children' (Liu and Chien 1998: 213).

Official attempts have been made to change this situation in Singapore by recent initiatives such as COMPASS (MOE 2005) that encourages schools to work more collaboratively with parents and the community. However, the actual percentage of parents who are actively involved in school activities remains small. There are several reasons for this. First, many parents work long hours outside the home, and have very little time to visit their children's schools or to participate in educational activities at home. Secondly, teaching has traditionally been seen as the responsibility of teachers and tutors who are paid for their services. Thirdly, parents who were educated in Chinese medium schools or are from lower income homes, and often have few academic qualifications, do not feel confident in speaking, reading or writing in the English language which is the main medium of instruction in Singapore schools. Despite these limitations there has been evidence that a greater number of Singapore parents wish to become more actively involved in their children's education (Sharpe 1991, 1996; Koo 1993; Quah et al. 1993; Clarke and Sharpe 2003).

Given the information about the potential pressures of the Singapore education system, the increased willingness by some parents to become more involved in their children's education, recent MOE initiatives to increase collaboration with parents and the weight of international research evidence reporting the benefits of parent involvement, it was considered timely to conduct the following study in Singapore.

The study focused on lower- and middle-income working parents, many of whom lacked the time, educational experience and confidence in the English language to become involved in their children's education. The aim was to investigate ways of empowering parents to become more actively involved in their children's learning and education during the final semester in preschool and during their transition to school. It was anticipated that their children's skills would improve more than a contrast group whose parents were less actively involved.

Getting Ready for School Project

This quasi-experimental study was conducted using a pre-test/post-test design (Campbell and Stanley 1963) to examine the effects of two parent involvement programmes. The study was conducted with 213 lower- and middle-income working parents and their children during the final six months in preschool. The sample was drawn from six childcare centres across Singapore. The study had several aims. One aim was to empower the parents by increasing their confidence and knowledge of their children's development, and the education system. A second aim was to increase the children's cognitive and language skills in preparation for starting school through working with their parents, rather than by preschool education alone.

The study compared the outcomes of two different methods of working with parents—parent and child interactive learning 'Guided Play' sessions (experimental group one), and parent-only evening workshops (experimental group two)—with a matched control/contrast group who received preschool education, but no additional parent sessions beyond the usual teacher–parent contacts for that preschool organization. The usual teacher–parent contacts in the six childcare centres included in the study were through daily face to face communication at delivery and collection time or through a home-school communication book, notes, emails or phone calls, and through the termly newsletter and parent–teacher conference.

A replication of the study was conducted in the following year with a new cohort of families in the same six childcare centres, but with treatments/interventions alternated (each childcare centre carried out a different parent intervention: guided play/parent workshops/control, than they had conducted the previous year) to counter any centre effects. The families were fully briefed about the intervention being conducted in their own child's centre and they signed a consent form if they wished to participate. They were not informed about the alternative interventions being conducted in the other centres in other parts of the island until the evaluation meetings at the end of the preschool phase of the study.

Method

The sample
The sample of 213 children and their parents were drawn from six childcare centres from a large, well-established childcare organization with 30 centres distributed across the whole of Singapore. This made it easier to control for possible centre effects in that they all shared the same policies and procedures, including identical home–school liaison practices, the same curriculum, facilities, teacher–child ratio, teaching techniques, timetabling and staff training. The six selected centres had a high percentage of lower and middle-income parents in full time employment.

The sample comprised 88 percent Chinese (national statistic 78%) and 12% from other races (Malay, Indian and Eurasian), which was 10% below national statistics. Sixty-four per cent of the parents used mainly Mother Tongue (Mandarin, Malay or Tamil) at home with the rest using a combination of English and Mother Tongue. Thirty-two per cent of the mothers, and 36% of the fathers had received primary or secondary education and had no formal qualifications, 54.5% of the mothers and 48% of the fathers held O-level, A-level or diploma qualifications, and 13.5% of the mothers and 18% of the fathers held graduate qualifications. Thirty-one per cent of the families had one child, 49% had two children, and 20% had three or four children. Sixty-nine per cent of the children in this study were the oldest child in the family and the first to enter school.

Two centres were randomly assigned to each of the three *conditions/interventions*, that is, experimental group one (guided play), experimental group two (parent workshops) and control/contrast group (no additional parent involvement sessions beyond those normally practised in the childcare centre as outlined above). There were no significant differences among the two experimental and one contrast group in terms of their ethnicity, income, parent's educational level and children's birth order (Pearson chi-square analysis). Therefore, the three groups were found to be well matched and outcomes most likely attributed to the additional parent involvement programmes.

Instruments and evaluation measures

Both quantitative and qualitative measures were used to answer the research questions using standardized tests (British Ability Scales (BAS II) Early Years and the Peabody Picture Vocabulary Test—Revised), school entry skills checklists (skills listed under five domains, with items based on the feedback of 60 P1, and 450 preschool teachers in Singapore) and language samples (running record of adult–child conversations), structured observations (child–parent interactions), questionnaires (parents, children and teachers), focus group discussions and individual interviews (parents and children).

Experimental Group One: guided play sessions (n = 83)

The organization of the Guided Play sessions was based on part of the daily routine Plan—Do—Review sequence, small group and adult–child activities of *High Scope* (The Perry Preschool, *High Scope* project, Schweinhart and Weikart 1985). It was considered that the Plan—Do—Review sequence would provide a clear structure in which teachers, children and parents could learn together. The curriculum, activity choices and the classroom layout were those used by the childcare organization, rather than that of High Scope. This was because the childcare organization had its own established curriculum, which had been devised to meet the preschool and local cultural needs, which was familiar to the teachers, children and parents participating in this study.

Parents and their children attended 10 Guided Play sessions, conducted on Saturday afternoons when the parents were not working. The sessions included:

- *Circle time*: in several small groups of about six children per group with their parents, and a preschool teacher to primarily sing action songs and rhymes.
- *Planning time*: children decide on three activities they wish to do and in which order. Parents and teacher write these onto record charts.
- *Doing time*: children and parents participated in the activities together, and are assisted by the preschool teachers as needed.
- *Review time*: children share what they had done in their small groups.
- *Story time*: teachers, parents or children read two stories, one in English and one in Chinese to the group.
- *Parents sharing session*: parents, teachers and the researcher discussed topical issues related to child development, and starting school including the school curriculum and pedagogies. Parents also shared the activities they completed at home with their children during the previous week. Meanwhile, the children participated in 'free-play' and selected books to take home to read with their parent's during the coming week.

Parents were given handouts for each session in English and, where possible, in Chinese, a copy of a 'Getting Ready for School' record and activity booklet, and a Reading Record booklet to record activities completed with their children. Each participating family compiled a portfolio of their child's activities completed during the Guided Play sessions, as well as at home.

Experimental Group Two: parent workshop sessions (n = 61)

Parents of children in the second experimental group attended six or seven workshop sessions (the non-Chinese parents did not attend the session on the teaching of Chinese in P1). The workshops were conducted during the evenings after work on a fortnightly basis. The topics covered childrearing practices, preparing children for starting school, the school curriculum and teaching techniques currently used in Singapore primary schools. Sessions on how to manage time, homework and children's behaviour were also included at the parents' request.

Parents received handouts for each session in English, and where possible, in Chinese, a copy of the 'Getting Ready for School' record and activity booklet, and the Reading Record booklet, which they could complete with their children at home. Locally produced videos and information leaflets in four languages (English, Chinese, Mandarin and Tamil) produced by the Ministry of Community Development Youth and Sports, were included in the sessions on 'Communicating with your child' and 'Managing stress and homework'. While a video by the Singapore Society for Reading and Literacy was used to demonstrate techniques for reading with young children. The locally produced videotapes were selected as it was thought that the parents would relate more to the Singapore context, rather than to 'western' examples.

Control/Contrast Group (n = 69)
The children in the two childcare centres assigned to the control/contrast group were receiving the full range of preschool services; however, their parents did not participate in any additional parent intervention sessions beyond those normally practiced in the childcare centre. The children in the contrast group completed the same pre- and post-test assessment as the two experimental groups. The children and parents in all groups were also interviewed and completed questionnaires at the beginning and end of the preschool project, and also participated in focus group discussions during the follow-up phase in P1. The parents in all the groups were also provided with information about their child's assessment results and current skills, and were advised about the skills requiring further development before school entry after they had completed the end of preschool project questionnaires.

Results

Pre- and post-test child outcomes
The effectiveness of the programmes was evaluated using mixed methodologies. The outcomes of the intervention groups were compared with the control/contrast group. The children's progress, and the level of their parents' confidence and support for their children's development and learning were measured before and after the 5-month intervention phase, and also at two points during the follow-up phase in Primary One. Statistical analysis of the quantitative data (ANOVA and ANCOVA) relating to the children's progress found significant results (p <0.01 and p <0.001) with the children in the parent intervention groups increasing in skills more than the contrast group by the end of the intervention in both years of the study. Minimal differences in outcomes were found between the two training methods ('guided play', parent and child interactive sessions, and the parent only workshop sessions), with both methods being equally effective in comparison with the control group.

Both the experimental groups had larger 'effect sizes' than did the control group on all language and academic measures each year. 'Effect size' describes how well the average student in one treatment group performed compared with the average student in another treatment group. It also measures the magnitude of their improvement between the pre- and post-tests (the effect size states the number of standard deviations that the post-test mean exceeds the pre-test mean). Borg and Gall (1989) considered effect sizes above 0.33 considered to have practical significance. For example the effect size between the 'guided play' and control groups ranged from 0.35 for reading test results to 0.94 for language comprehension test results. The effect size between the parent workshop and control groups ranged from 0.41 for reading to 0.91 for number skills.

Pre- and post-test parent outcomes

The quantitative dependent variables relating to parents such as knowledge of their child's strengths and weaknesses, levels of participation in activities with their child, and levels of confidence in being able to assist their child's learning were tested for significance among the groups by chi-square analysis. Qualitative data relating to parents were summarized by themes and patterns, percentages calculated and examples cited. Changes in parent–child interactions during the Guided Play sessions were analysed by individual cases. Analysis of the quantitative and qualitative data found significant group differences between the outcomes of intervention groups ('guided play' parent and child interactive sessions, and the parent only workshop sessions) and the contrast group.

Parents in both intervention groups had increased significantly in their knowledge about their children's skills and the skills required for primary school. The parents in the intervention groups had also increased significantly in their confidence in assisting their child's learning and education. They also completed significantly more educational activities at home compared with the contrast group by the end of the project. There were minor differences between the two experimental groups at the end of the intervention phase, with the parents in the 'guided play' group reporting higher levels of confidence, reading more often with their children, and teaching them how to plan and organize their time compared with the 'parent workshop' group. However, overall minimal differences in outcomes were found between the two intervention methods, with both being equally effective compared with the control/contrast group.

When parents were asked to evaluate the usefulness of the interventions the majority cited knowing what to expect in Primary One and learning how to teach their child specific skills as the most useful [77% of the Guided Play (GP) group and 64% of the Parent Workshop (PW) group]. Forty per cent of the GP group and 34% of the PW group cited having gained better knowledge of their own child through observation and increased interaction, while 27% of the GP group and 15% of the PW group said that the project had enabled them to spend more quality time with their child. Forty per cent of the parents offered improvement suggestions and most of these related to the need to start the sessions earlier in the year, and to extend the number and duration of the sessions.

Follow-up in Primary One

A follow-up during the first year in primary school found that the majority of children from all three groups had adjusted well to Primary One. The differences in the children's skills between the experimental and control group children were measured by school exam results, and teachers ratings of class and homework, and social interaction skills. The significant differences between the children's academic and language skills between the treatment and contrast groups at the end of preschool had not been maintained in Primary One (P1). However, the social and interaction skills of the children who had participate in the guided play groups were rated higher than the other two groups.

Parents and children completed follow-up questionnaires in the middle and at the end of P1, and participated in focus group discussions in mid-year. The differences between the intervention group and control group parents in terms of their knowledge, child rearing practices and confidence that were measured at the post-intervention stage at the end of preschool, were not maintained to the same degree by the follow-up stage in P1. However, one difference related to the supervision of homework and studying at home, with fewer parents from the guided play group hiring tuition teachers than the other two groups. Parents were generally happy with their children's schools although they expressed more concerns when participating in the focus group discussions compared with their individually completed questionnaire responses.

Fifty six per cent of the parents and children attended the focus groups, which were held in their previous preschool centres. Although there were no real differences in the content of the discussions across the three groups, the parents in the two experimental groups made more comments and gave more improvement suggestions. Overall, the parents considered that their children had settled well into school and that the teaching was acceptable; however, they had a number of concerns.

Parents expressed concern about insufficient home–school communication and relationships with teachers, with parents not feeling as informed or included as they had been in preschool. Concern was also expressed about some primary school teachers described by parents as 'fierce' or insensitive to their children's vulnerabilities and about some school organization issues. The organizational issues were mainly about homework and health matters, such as heavy school bags, and that some teachers did not allow children to drink water or visit the toilet during lesson time. The parents who had participated in the two intervention groups were able to make very practical suggestions for primary schools, preschools and for the research project.

Conclusions for the Getting Ready for School study

This quasi-experimental study conducted during the last semester in pre-school had significant beneficial effects by the end of preschool on both the parents and children in the two intervention groups compared with the control/contrast group. The increase in the knowledge, skills, self-confidence and ability of parents to express their needs, particularly in the parent–child interaction groups (guided play), has been linked to parent empowerment (for example, Wolfendale 1992; Pizzo 1993; Pugh et al. 1994; Alexander 1997; Pugh 1999a,b). The hypothesis that this increase would lead to improvements in their children's skills was also proven.

However, differences between the intervention and control/contrast groups, particularly in children's academic achievements, had reduced by the end of the first year in primary school. This has been found by many other early intervention studies (for example, Hebbeler 1985; McKey et al. 1985; Barnett and Escobar 1990; Slavin et al. 1994; Barnett 1995). It is possible that the intensity and duration of the interventions was insufficient to bring about lasting change as noted by Karweit and Wasik (1994) when identifying key indicators of success from a meta-analysis of early intervention programmes in the USA. The need for continuity in parent involvement and support during lower primary school has also been widely reported in similar studies in the USA, for example by Slavin et al. (1994).

Feedback during their children's first year in school indicated that they generally coped well with the changed demands. However, many parents expressed concern that there was insufficient home–school liaison and in-sufficient guidance in how to assist children with their homework. Parents from homes where little English was used experienced the most difficulties.

Recommendations

There were several recommendations as a result of this study. Firstly, in-creasing parent involvement during the preschool years and transition to school was recommended as beneficial for all concerned. Secondly, it was recommended that particular attention be given to empowering the parents from lower income and non-English speaking groups. Concern was expressed, however, about singling out this group of parents for intervention as a se-parate group as this might 'ghettoize' them, causing disempowerment by labelling them as 'inadequate'. The beneficial effects of having 'mixed' parent groups, by language, social and educational experience, where parents can learn from one another's experiences and strengths was recommended. Fur-ther studies to empower parents by different techniques are clearly required and especially to compare whether workshops alone or parent–child interactive sessions are more effective in terms of parent and child outcomes. Thirdly, the need to increase parent involvement during primary schools was recommended in order to maintain the benefits of parent involvement programmes during preschool.

The results of this study were disseminated to the Ministry of Education through a report, and to preschool and primary school teachers during conferences, seminars and workshop sessions. Many preschool centres are now including a variety of activities to increase parent involvement in their centres and through take-home activities. It is important that teachers receive training and support in how to conduct their own research to evaluate changed practices and so learn from 'evidence-based practice' (Potter 2001). It is hoped that this will be facilitated by many of the preschool training programmes in Singapore now including a research methods and action-research project module.

There is also a need for further research to investigate transition during the first year in school and particularly focusing on parent involvement during this process. As noted earlier, parent involvement practices in primary schools are more variable. There have been several initiatives reported in publications by COMPASS, but these have not yet been evaluated. Clearly, evaluation studies into parent involvement throughout the primary school years are also required.

Further transition studies have subsequently been undertaken by the author and other colleagues at the National Institute of Education focusing on children's first year in primary school in Singapore. Results of these studies plan to be published later in 2006.

References

Alexander, T. (1997) *Empowering Parents: Families as the Foundation of a Learning Society*. London: National Children Bureau.

Alexander, K.L. and Entwisle, D.R. (1988) Facilitating the transition to first grade: The nature of transition and research on factors affecting it, *Elementary School Journal*, 98(4): 351–64.

Barnett, W.S. (1995) Long-term effects of early childhood programmes on cognitive and school outcomes, *Future of Children*, 5(3): 25–50.

Barnett, W.S. and Escobar, C.M. (1990) Economic costs and benefits of early intervention, in S. J. Meisels and J. P. Shonkoff (eds) *Handbook of Early Childhood Intervention*. Cambridge: Cambridge University Press.

Borg, R.W. and Gall, M.D. (1989) *Educational Research. An Introduction*, 5th edn. White Plains: Longman

Campbell, D.T. and Stanley, J.C. (1963) *Experimental and Quasi-experimental Designs for Research*. Chicago: McNally.

Clarke, C. (2000) *The Effects of Parent Training Programmes on Children's Preparedness for School and on Parent's Support of Children's Development and Learning in School*, Academic Research Fund Report. Singapore: Singapore National Institute of Education.

Clarke, C. and Sharpe, P. J. (2003) Transition from preschool to primary school: an overview of the personal experiences of children and their parents in Singapore, *European Early Childhood Research Monographs*, Series No. 1: 15–33.

Chen, C. and Stevenson, H. W. (1989) Homework: a cross-cultural examination, *Child Development*, 60: 551–61.

Cleave, S., Jowett, S. and Bate, M. (1982) *And so to School. A Study of Continuity from Preschool to Infant School*. Windsor: NFER-Nelson.

Crystal, D.S. and Stevenson, H.W. (1991) Mothers' perceptions of children's problems with mathematics: a cross-national comparison, *Journal of Educational Psychology*, 83(3): 372–6.

Docket, S. and Perry, B. (2004) Starting school: perspectives of Australian children, parents and educators, *Journal of Early Childhood Research*, 2(2): 171–89.

Dornbusch, S., Ritter, P., Leiderman, P.H., Roberts, D. and Fraleigh, M. (1987) The relation of parenting style to adolescent school performance, *Child Development*, 58: 1244–57.

Epstein, J.L. (1995) School, family, community partnerships: caring for the children we share, *Phi Delta Kappan*, 76: 701–12.

Fan-Eng, M.W.Y. and Sharpe, P.E. (2000) Characteristics of preschool environments and teachers effectiveness in selected child care centres, in C. Tan-Niam and M. L. Quah (eds) *Investing in our Future: The Early Years*. Singapore: McGraw-Hill.

Gan L. (2004) Marrying preschool and early primary programmes to ensure effective transition—recent policy and pedagogical shifts in Singapore. Paper presented at the EECERA 14th Annual Conference, Malta, 1–4 September, 2004.

Gordon, I.J. (1969) Developing parent power, in E. Grotberg (ed.) *Critical Issues in Research Related to Disadvantaged Children*. Princeton, NJ. Educational Testing Service.

Gordon, T. (1977) Parent education and parent involvement: retrospective and prospect, *Childhood Education*, 54: 71–9.

Hebbeler, K. (1985) An old and a new question on the effects of early education for children from low income homes, *Educational Evaluation and Policy Analysis*, 7: 207–16.

Hinton, S. (1989) Dimensions of parental involvement: easing the transfer from preschool to primary, in S. Wolfendale (ed.) *Parent Involvement: Developing Networks Between School, Home and Community*. London: Cassell.

Johansson, I. (2002) Parent's views of transition to school and their influence in this process, in H. Fabian and A-W. Dunlop (eds) *Transitions in the Early Years*. London: RoutledgeFalmer,

Karweit, B.A. and Wasik, N.L. (1994) Off to a good start: effects of birth to three interventions on early school success, in R. E. Slavin, B. A. Karweit and N. L. Wasik (eds) *Preventing Early School Failure. Research, Policy and Practice*. Boston: Allyn and Bacon.

Ko, P.S. and Ho, W.K. (1992) *Growing up in Singapore. The Pre-school Years*. Singapore: Longman.

Koo, G.C. (1993) *Parents as Catalyst: The Role of Parents in the Development of the Young Child in Asia*, workshop report. Opening address in RTRC Asia, UNICEF, and Save the Children conference: Child Survival and Development, Singapore, UNICEF.

Kwan, C. (2000) Using the early childhood environment rating scale in Singapore, in C. Tan-Niam and M. L. Quah (eds) *Investing in our Future: The Early Years*. Singapore: McGraw-Hill.

Kwan, C. (2001) Looking at quality indicators in childcare centres, *Teaching and Learning* 22(2): 93–106.

Kwan, C., Sylva, K. and Reeves, B. (1998) Day care quality and child development in Singapore, *Early Child Development and Care*, 144: 69–77.

Lam, H.M.Y. (1999) A study of Hong Kong parents' views on kindergarten education, *Early Child Development and Care*, 159: 17–24.

Lim, A.S.E. (1994) Relationship of play and language patterns among Singaporean preschool children in homes and classrooms, *International Journal of Early Years Education*, 2(2): 65–91.

Liu K.C.Y. and Chu-Ying Chien (1998) Project approach and parent involvement in Taiwan, *Childhood Education*, summer: 213–19.

Maxwell, K.L. and Eller, S.K. (1994) Children's transition to kindergarten, *Young Children*, September: 56–63.

McKey, R.H., Condelli, L., Ganson H., Barrett, B.J., McConkey, C. and Plantz, M.C. (1985) *The Impact of Head Start on Children, Families and Communities*, final report of the Head Start Evaluation, Synthesis and Utilization Project. Washington, DC: CSR.

Ministry of Community Development, Youth and Sports (2005) Available at: http:// www.mcds.gov.sg

Ministry of Education (2005) *Preschool*. Available at: http:// www1.moe.edu.sg/ preschooleducation.

Ministry of Education & COMPASS (2005) Available at: http:// www1.moe.edu.sg/ pgsb/compass/htm.

Ng, S-W. (2000) The impact of social class differences on parent involvement in school education in Hong Kong, *Educational Journal*, 28(2): 35–62.

Parr, J., McNaughton, S., Timberley, H. and Robinson, V. (1993) Bridging the gap: practices of collaboration between home and the junior school, *Australian Journal of Early Childhood*, 18(3): 35–42.

Perry, B., Dockett, S. and Howard, P. (2000) Starting school: issues for children, parents and teachers, *Journal of Australian Research in Early Childhood Education*, 7(1): 41–53.

Pizzo, P.D. (1993) Parent empowerment and child care regulation, *Young Children*, September: 9–12.

Potter, G. (2001) Facilitating critical reflection on practice through collaborative research, *Australian Educational Researcher*, 28(3): 117–39.

Pugh, G. (1999a) Parenting education and the Social Policy agenda, in S. Wolfendale, and H. Einzig (eds) *Parenting Education and Support. New Opportunities*. London: David Fulton.

Pugh, G. (1999b) Young children and their families: creating a community response, in L. Abbott, and H. Moylett (eds) *Early Education Transformed*. London: Falmer Press.

Pugh, G. and De'Ath, E. (1989) *Working towards Partnership in the Early Years*. London: National Children's Bureau.

Pugh, G., De'Ath, E. and Smith, C. (1994) *Confident Parents, Confident Children: Policy and Practice in Parent Education and Support*. London: National Children's Bureau.

Quah, M.L., Sharpe, P., Lim, S.E. and Heng, M.A. (1993) Home Environment and Parental Involvement as determinants of Attainment Among Lower Primary School Children in Singapore. Paper presented at the Singapore Principals' Conference, 5–8 September, 1993.

Raban, B. and Ure, C. (2000) Continuity for socially disadvantaged school entrants: perspectives of parents and teachers, *Journal of Australian Research in Early Childhood Education*, 7(1): 54–65.

Retas, S. and Kwan, C. (2000) Preschool quality and staff characteristics in Singapore, in C. Tan-Niam and M.L. Quah (eds) *Investing in our Future: the Early Years*. Singapore: McGraw-Hill.

Seng, S.H. (1994) Quality kindergarten education in Singapore: parents' views and expectations. Paper presented at 13th Biennial meetings of International Society for the Study of Behavioural Development. Amsterdam, Netherlands, June 29–July 2 1994.

Seng, S.H. and Lazar, I. (1992) Early childhood education in Singapore, in S. Feeney (ed.) *Early Childhood Education in Asia and the Pacific* New York: Garland.

Sharpe, P.J. (1991) Parental involvement in pre-schools: parents' and teachers' perceptions of their roles, *Early Child Development and Care*, 71: 53–62.

Sharpe, P.J. (1994) A study of some of the environmental features found to be conducive to the bilingual development of preschool children in Singapore, *Early Child Development and Care*, 98: 59–72.

Sharpe, P.J. (1996) Determinants of preschool quality in Singapore. An investigation of the effects on teachers, of parents' involvement, *International Journal of Early Years Education*, 4(1): 47–63.

Sharpe P.J. (1997) Teaching and learning at home. Features of bilingual support for the bilingual competence of pre-schoolers, *Early Child Development and Care*, 130: 75–83.

Sharpe, P.J. (2002a) Some developments in preschool education in Singapore. Paper presented at the QCA International seminar, Early Years Education: An International Perspective, Oxford, 13–15 February 2002.

Sharpe, P.J. (2002b) Preparing for primary school in Singapore—Aspects of adjustment to the more formal demands of the Primary One mathematics syllabus, *Early Child Development and Care*, 172(4): 329–35.

Sharpe, P.J. (2003) *A new curriculum for kindergarten children in Singapore*. Singapore: ASCD Review.

Slavin, R.E., Karweit, N.L. and Wasik, B.A. (1994) *Preventing Early School Failure, Research, Policy and Practice*. Boston: Allyn and Bacon.

Steinberg, L., Mounts, N., Lamborn, S. and Dornbush, S. (1991) Authoritative parenting and adolescent adjustment across various ecological niches, *Journal of Research on Adolescence*, 1: 19–36.

Sue, S. and Okazaki, S. (1990) Asian-American educational achievements: a phenomenon in search of an explanation, *American Psychologist*, 45: 913–20.

Schweinhart, L.J. and Weikart, D.P. (1985) Evidence that good early childhood programs work. Phi Delta Kappan, 66, 8.

Tan-Niam, C.S.L. (1994) Thematic fantasy play: effects on the perspective-taking of preschool children, *International Journal of Early Years Education*, 2(1): 5–16.

Wolfendale, S. (1992) *Empowering Parents and Teachers: Working for Children*. London: Cassell.

Yeo L.S. and Clarke, C. (2005) Starting school—a Singapore Story. *Australian Journal of Early Childhood*. Vol 30 No 3 pp 1–9.

10 Expectations: effects of curriculum change as viewed by children, parents and practitioners

Margaret Stephenson and Margaret Parsons

The transition from home or preschool setting to formal school has been the focus of increased attention in recent years. Much valuable work has been done which seeks to identify ways to make this as positive an experience as possible for children (for example, Dockett and Perry 2001; Dockett and Perry 2002; Fabian 2002, Fabian and Dunlop 2002). A successful start to school is seen as important because of the long-term benefits to learning that this can have, and the need to plan the transition in such a way as to ensure continuity and progression is well documented (Fabian 2002). However, there is an increasing recognition that the way in which the transition from one stage of learning to another is managed and organized must be better explored and understood. Young children in England experience a significant transition when they reach the end of their first full year in primary school, when they move from the Foundation Stage to Key Stage One of the National Curriculum. This signifies a major change in children's experience within the school environment but passes almost unnoticed (Parsons and Stephenson 2002). The transition from the Foundation Stage to Key Stage One of the National Curriculum entails a fundamental shift in the curriculum that young children experience. The Foundation Stage promotes a curriculum that encompasses 'everything children do, see, hear or feel in their setting, both planned and unplanned' (QCA/Department for Education and Employment 2000: 1), this may not only involve changes in the activities and experiences young children engage in, but also changes in the learning environment, approaches to teaching and learning, relationships with adults and assessment. There is potential here for disruption and loss of continuity in learning at a very young age. This chapter will explore this transition and consider the implications for children's development as learners if it is not managed effectively.

Background

The introduction of the Foundation Stage took place within a context of increasing government investment in children and families since the election of the first New Labour government in 1997. This proved to be very significant for families, children and practitioners. For the first time, the state acknowledged that it had a responsibility to its youngest citizens and, subsequently, the government has invested heavily in childcare and education (Jackson 2004) and the introduction of the Foundation Stage in September 2000 came as part of this investment. The Foundation Stage (QCA/Department for Education and Employment 2000) offers children a curriculum that addresses six areas of learning: personal, social and emotional development, communication, language and literacy, mathematical development, knowledge and understanding of the world, physical development and creative development (QCA/Department for Education and Employment 2000). The inclusion of personal, social and emotional development recognizes that all aspects of children's development are important, not just the cognitive. The provision of an environment that supports learning and opportunities for the child to be an active participant in their learning, are implicit in the guidance published for practitioners (QCA/Department for Education and Employment 2000). The emphasis on the integration of play and learning has also been welcomed (Wood 2004), and it is acknowledged that the Foundation Stage has the potential to meet children's needs in a stimulating and appropriate way (Jackson 2004).

The Foundation Stage has also allayed some concerns about the place of 4-year-olds in school. In the latter years of the twentieth century, there was increasing unease in the early years community about the number of 4-year-old children being admitted to schools. Research highlighted the inappropriateness of provision in some Reception classes. Staff with inadequate training to teach young children and concern that the curriculum was not appropriate for young children, were just two of the concerns raised (Cleave and Brown 1991; Bennett et al. 1997). The Foundation Stage ensures the entitlement of all 4-year-olds in school to access a curriculum that is appropriate to their needs. New consultation on the *Early Years Foundation Stage (EYFS) single quality framework for services to children from birth to five* (Department for Education and Skills 2006), promises to ensure that access to appropriate curriculum remains on the agenda.

At the end of the Reception year, children move into Year One and this marks the formal beginning of their involvement with the National Curriculum. The National Curriculum is based on a view of learning that is in sharp contrast to the Foundation Stage. The curriculum is divided into specific subjects and the content is prescribed in the form of attainment targets.

Children and teachers must also meet the demands of an assessment procedure, which seeks to measure children's progress in meeting these targets: schools are accountable to parents, Local Education Authorities and society at large for the results of this testing. In a context where practice is 'oriented towards achieving defined objectives' (Wood 2004: 19), the approaches to teaching and learning that are employed by practitioners at Key Stage One may be very different to those used by practitioners in the Foundation Stage. It must be remembered that the children experiencing these changes may be as young as five. The curriculum may change abruptly, but children do not; 5-year-olds whose birth date precipitates them into working in the context of Year One have the same needs and rights as those in the Foundation Stage. The way that this transition is managed, and the manner in which children are introduced to the new curriculum and all its attendant changes are both of great importance.

How and when does the transition between curricula take place?

The transition from the Foundation Stage to Key Stage One of the National Curriculum involves discontinuities that occur in a number of areas, including the environment, social relationships, expectations and curriculum content. Bronfenbrenner (1979) describes this multilayered change as an ecological shift and accompanying this ecological shift the child will experience a shift in expectation, both as a social member of the class group and as a learner. Adjustment to a new situation may demand a consideration of all aspects of the ecological shift which impinge upon the child (Dunlop 2003) or require a stabilizing of one aspect of the shift, as Ladd suggests in his consideration of the value of maintaining friendships through a transition (Ladd 1990).

Bronfenbrenner (1979) offers a model that enables us to analyse the changes taking place during the transition period. The view the child takes of the transition will be influenced by those who share the immediate ecological environment, or microsystem, and are close to the child, such as parents and teachers. The child is also affected by situations in which he/she takes part (mesosystems), and by decisions and events that take place outside of the child's environment, and of which he/she has no knowledge or control (exosystems) (Bronfenbrenner 1979). The child involved in the transition will directly experience change in his/her activities and environment. The expectations of those who have influence over the child, in this case parents and teachers, also undergo change. The requirements and expectations of the wider community such as the Local Education Authority and government curriculum requirements will cause a shift in the view of the teacher which in turn may affect the child's view of him/herself as a learner.

Teachers work within wider school communities, which develop their own ethos and their own particular policies for the way in which transitions are managed. Yeboah (2002) suggests that it is important for institutions to implement policies that clearly define what is expected of children in different phases of education. OFSTED (2004) found that at best, the management of transition at this stage of a child's education was part of a whole school approach to achieving good curricular continuity and progression in learning. However, Seefeldt et al. (1997, cited by Yeboah 2002) claim that it is usual practice for plans and policies to be developed that seek to impose on children the ideas, beliefs and values of the educator, rather than on what children know and understand. For English schools, these ideas, beliefs and values are determined to a large extent by the expectations of central government. The current educational climate in England emphasizes raising standards and has resulted in the introduction of heavily prescribed national strategies for literacy and numeracy. Progress towards raising standards is measured by national testing at 7 and 11, the results of which are made public in the form of league tables. Being seen to be successful in this testing process may be what determines plans and policies for many English schools.

Schools and teachers have to mediate government policy and their own philosophy. Research has shown that this mediation can be problematic. In 1989, the Early Years Curriculum Group found that teachers were experiencing tension between sustaining the established principles of effective early years practice in the face of the demands of the National Curriculum (Early Years Curriculum Group 1989). The structure and requirements of the Foundation Stage sow the seeds of this tension. Although the Foundation Stage covers the period to the end of the reception year, the areas of learning relating to Communication Language and Literacy, and Mathematical Development are in line with the objectives found in National frameworks for teaching literacy and mathematics in the reception year (Department for Education and Employment 1998, 1999). The strategy documents contain curriculum guidance designed to help reception teachers plan using these objectives. The guidance advises teachers that they do not need to cover the elements of the literacy hour and daily mathematics lesson in one unit of time. Teachers are also advised to adopt an approach to teaching and learning that is playful in nature (Department for Education and Employment 1998: 108; Department for Education and Employment 1999: 27). However, there is concern that the requirements to begin work on the strategies may have a detrimental effect upon the content and teaching approach in the Reception class and that children are being moved too soon from a play-based curriculum to a subject-based curriculum (McInnes 2002; Cooper and Sixsmith 2003). As children move through to the end of the Foundation Stage, in order to accommodate the increasing subject-based approach, whole class teaching and the organization of children in ability groups can become more common, to the detriment of more creative and active areas of the curriculum (David 2003).

Why practitioners working in Reception classes feel it necessary to move towards a more formal approach to teaching and learning is an aspect of practice that merits research, but it may possibly be attributed to lack of confidence or knowledge in how to teach literacy and numeracy through play (David 2003). Perceptions of what OFSTED inspectors might expect to see may also contribute to these developments as OFSTED takes the view that there is a universal definition of quality: this does not acknowledge that the needs and interests of different contexts and cultures might be significant in shaping provision (Anning et al. 2004). Research (Bennett et al. 1997) has also shown that, whilst expressing a belief in learning through play, for example, the practice of teachers does not always reflect this belief. Could the National Curriculum be an excuse for not adopting certain approaches to teaching and learning that are associated with effective early years practice? Perhaps most significantly, OFSTED (2004) found that teachers recognize that children need to be prepared for national tests in Year Two and, in practice, this led to preparation for testing beginning in the latter part of the Reception year. Whatever the reason, the transition to a more formal curriculum may be taking place in some classrooms before the end of the Reception year, and there is evidence of the emergence of an accepted pedagogical formula for literacy and numeracy in particular (David 2003). Kelly (2004) points out that a distinction between what is taught and how it is taught is difficult to make; the implication of this is that if one is prescribed, then freedom in the other may also be eroded.

When children move to Year One, they begin to experience the full range of the National Curriculum. Parsons and Stephenson (2002) found that preparation for this move could be minimal. Children may make visits to the Year One classroom to become familiar with their new environment and to meet their new teacher. They may spend an afternoon in the new classroom and this was also found by OFSTED (2004). However, the change in the curriculum was not explained to children and there were no discussions about how the kinds of activities that children would be doing might change. Reception teachers may also begin to introduce more formal ways of teaching as preparation for the transition. Even the most extensive preparation did not match the work done by Reception teachers at the beginning of the first year of compulsory school and schools had no formal policy about how to approach this change.

It would not be appropriate to suggest that the National Curriculum is not concerned with the development of the whole child or with processes of learning. However, the subject-based approach it adopts is a significant difference and, although there is an expectation of continuity (Cooper and Sixsmith 2003), a recent evaluation by HMI of the transition from the Reception Year to Year One found that the subject-based approach of the National Curriculum has been interpreted insensitively by many Year One teachers and that timetable issues and the need to ensure good progress towards standards expected at the end of Key Stage One tests lead to an abrupt transition to formal approaches (OFSTED 2004). David (2003) cites evidence suggesting that in Key Stage One there is a move towards controlled, defined or dictated forms of pedagogy. Changes may also occur in the range of subjects offered to children in Year One: OFSTED (2004: 2) found that, in some Year One classes, the curriculum emphasizes literacy and numeracy 'at the expense of regular attention to other subjects' and that, as a result, there is an imbalance in the Year One curriculum. A lack of clear transitional links between the Foundation Stage curriculum and National Curriculum subjects (OFSTED 2004) does not help teachers to manage the transition in a way that would be more appropriate for young children. This contrasts with other countries such as the French Community of Belgium and Sweden, where stronger links across age groups and settings have been developed (Neuman 2002).

Teachers in the Foundation Stage can lack confidence and/or the appropriate training, we find the situation is no different in Key Stage One. The development of the notion that early years education in England covers the age range 3–5 years is not helpful in this respect. Children in Key Stage One of the National Curriculum, who are aged 5–7 years, are as much 'early years' as their peers in Reception classes. However, training and continuing professional development in appropriate practice for early years is confined to teachers in the Foundation Stage. It is not surprising, therefore, that teachers in Years One and Two may feel that a formal approach to the curriculum is inappropriate for some children in their care, but do not feel equipped to address this issue. The National Curriculum, and other demands and expectations, may then become a means of avoiding a potentially difficult issue.

Parents

When children move from preschool settings or home to compulsory school, parents are often a key part of this transition. Links between home and school, and collaboration between parents and teachers is an integral part of the transition (Margetts 2002). Margetts (2002) stresses the importance of parents being informed about schools' expectations and procedures when children start school as information can reduce parental stress about the changes children will experience; this makes them better able to support children. The transition to a new curriculum also leads to many changes in a child's experiences at school, and these may lead to frustration and confusion. However, the transition from Foundation Stage to Key Stage One may not be characterized by the same degree of parental involvement (Parsons and Stephenson 2002) as the move from home to school. OFSTED (2004) found that parents were informed about curriculum topics and plans, and about routines and expectations. Good practice of this kind needs to be extended, because if parents are excluded from knowledge of the changes children may be experiencing and the new demands that are being made upon them, they may not be in a strong position from which to support children's learning.

Parents' expectations of what children should be doing at school is another important aspect of this transition. OFSTED (2004) found that parents expected to see changes in Year One from structured play-based activities to more formal teaching and learning, including a sharper focus on reading, writing and number. Parents can seem to consistently prefer education of this nature (MacNaughton 2003). What parents perceive as being important for young children may be in conflict with what practitioners think is appropriate and tension can arise.

Implications for children

There are many implications for children arising from the move from a curriculum that emphasizes the need for children to 'explore, experiment, plan and make decisions for themselves' (QCA/Department for Education and Employment 2000: 12) to one that emphasizes measuring achievement against predetermined outcomes. In particular, we believe that this transition has an impact on the development of children as learners. Going to school is not just about the 'accumulation of particular bodies of knowledge, skill and understanding' (Claxton and Carr 2004: 91). It is also about developing 'long-term learning trajectories' (Claxton and Carr 2004: 91). In 1998, the United Kingdom government produced a document entitled 'The learning age: a renaissance for a new age' (Department for Education and Employment 1998, cited in Hargreaves 2004) in which a vision of a culture of lifelong learning was set out. If this vision is to be achieved, then the 'motivation and capacity to learn' (Hargreaves 2004: 10) must be established and school is the context in which children's growth as a learner for life begins. It is in continuing to strengthen dispositions for learning across their school career that children will emerge as effective learners for life. Katz suggests that dispositions 'can be thought of as habits of the mind, tendencies to respond to situations in certain ways' (Katz 1988, cited in Carr 2001). Carr (2001) proposes five domains of learning dispositions: taking an interest; being involved; persisting with difficulty or uncertainty; communicating with others and taking responsibility. This forms the basis of a model that can be used to monitor and assess the active involvement of the child in a specific context within the learning environment. Claxton and Carr (2004) further define disposition in terms of progress, breadth: allowing a child to transfer a successful approach from one learning situation to another, and richness: relating to the increasingly mature application of questioning or collaboration, so that disposition is not acquired, but developed and what is important is the degree to which that development takes place. The link between developing a disposition, learning and the role of the teacher is such that disposition becomes a growing entity, which forms part of lifelong learning. Using these definitions a disposition to learn becomes more than motivation or a willingness to engage, but necessitates the development of a wide range of social, personal and intellectual skills, which will ultimately enable the child to deepen and intensify the learning experience.

Claxton and Carr (2004) suggest that different types of learning communities may at one extreme prohibit opportunities to develop certain dispositions, such as persistence and engagement over time, and at the other may empower children to develop actively and extend dispositions for learning. MacNaughton (2003) identifies different curricula, which can either disempower children and make them passive learners, or which give children a much more active part in determining their own learning.

Early exposure to a curriculum built on observable and testable learning outcomes, such as the National Curriculum, delivered in a structured and formal manner creates a context in which children are potentially disempowered, and in which they may be made passive and may not be the most appropriate context in which children develop dispositions for learning. Nabuco and Sylva (1996, cited in Anning et al. 2004) showed how 'over formal' approaches to teaching young children are counter-productive, and can create anxiety and low self-esteem. An anxious child who does not regard him or herself as capable is unlikely to risk engaging in activities that will strengthen dispositions for learning. An assessment system that focuses on identifying whether children have or have not achieved specific skills and knowledge may also have an effect on children's views of themselves as learners. The Foundation Stage profile, which assesses young children's progress in the very earliest years of school is focused on 13 assessment scales, each containing nine points for assessment. The aim of the profile is to provide a summary of a child's achievements based on accumulated observations and knowledge of the child acquired by practitioners during the Foundation Stage. Although based on the sound principle of assessment through observation, the profile has met with resistance (Anning et al. 2004). It does carry with it implications of failure; a child who does not achieve all nine points in each scale may be deemed to have fallen short of the norm and risks being labelled as an underachiever before his/her time in Key Stage One has begun. Once in Year One, the emphasis on assessment in core subjects of

English, Mathematics and Science begins, and the notion of evaluating children as learners has been lost. However, the introduction of the new Primary National Strategy, which emphasizes progression in aspects of learning for young children, may address this issue in future.

A curriculum in which children are able to explore their own interests delivered in a more flexible way will provide an environment more conducive to the development of learning dispositions. Curriculum guidance for the Foundation Stage encourages practitioners to promote a positive attitude and disposition to learn, through a curriculum that gives children an opportunity to plan and initiate their own activities, with time to become engrossed, work in depth and complete activities. Wenger (1998) suggests that the ability of a child to maintain and develop an identity as a learner is more important than the demonstration that a predetermined curriculum has been achieved. He further suggests that when schools do not offer children the opportunity to engage in identification and negotiability, the child appears unwilling or unable to learn. The move to a curriculum that denies these opportunities may have a detrimental affect on children's perception of themselves as learners and on the degree to which they continue to develop dispositions for learning. OFSTED (2004) acknowledges that the practical experiences and opportunities for structured play allowed children to achieve early success and to develop confidence as learners. This confidence and success is vital if children are to maintain their perception of themselves as effective learners and to develop the dispositions that will allow them to continue to learn.

There is a real risk, therefore, that the transition from the Foundation Stage to Key Stage One of the National Curriculum and all this entails could potentially constrain the development of children's dispositions for learning, rather than sustain and nurture them. Dunlop (2004) has found that children who are creative, fluent and capable often experience a loss of confidence in the first days, weeks and months at school. There is a danger that a similar dip in confidence may occur at this point in a child's school career and an inappropriate approach to teaching and learning in Key Stage One may not enable this to be restored. In a climate where lifelong learning forms an integral part of the government's vision for education, it is vital to recognize that the foundations of this are laid in schools (Hargreaves 2004) and that the first few years in school will play an important part in developing children as learners. It is vital, therefore, that schools pay more attention to ways in which the transition from the Foundation Stage curriculum to Key Stage One is approached and managed. Perhaps the most valuable contribution that could be made to the development of children as learners in their first years in school would be to abandon completely the notion that 'early years' ends at five. Much could be learnt from the approach that the Welsh National Assembly has taken; in Wales, testing at 7 is to be abolished, and the Foundation Stage will be extended to include children up to the age of 7. This move is based on research evidence that suggests that 'children do not begin to benefit from extensive formal teaching until about the age of 6 or 7, in line with their social and cognitive development. An earlier introduction can result in some children underachieving and attaining lower standards' (Welsh National Assembly 2004). Whilst there is still reference to standards, there is an acknowledgement that hurrying children into formal learning in order to meet whatever standards are set is not the answer. A longer period, in a context that allows children to strengthen their dispositions for learning, will better equip children with the tools needed to show resilience in the face of change to a more formal curriculum.

References

Anning, A., Cullen, J. and Fleer, M (2004) Research contexts across cultures, in A. Anning, J. Cullen and M. Fleer (eds) *Early Childhood Education. Society and Culture*. London: Sage.

Bennett, N., Wood, L. and Rogers, S. (1997) *Teaching Through Play. Teachers' Thinking and Classroom Practice*. Buckingham: University Press.

Bronfenbrenner, U. (1979) *The Ecology of Human Development. Experiments by Nature and Design*. Cambridge: Harvard University Press.

Carr, M. (2001) *Assessment in Early Childhood Settings. Learning Stories*. London: Sage Publications.

Claxton, G. and Carr, M. (2004) A framework teaching and learning the dynamics of disposition, *Early Years*, 24(1). pp. 87–97.

Cleave, S. and Brown, S. (1991) *Four Year Olds in School: Quality Matters*. Slough: National Foundation for Educational Research.

Cooper, H. and Sixsmith, C. (2003) *Teaching Across the Early Years 3–7. Curriculum Coherence And Continuity*. London: RoutledgeFalmer,

David, T. (2003) *Early Years Research: Pedagogy, Curriculum and Adult Roles, Training and Professionalism*. Southwell: British Educational Research Association.

Department for Education and Employment (1998) *The National Literacy Strategy*. London: Department for Education and Employment.

Department for Education and Employment (1999) *The National Numeracy Strategy*. London: Department for Education and Employment.

Department for Education and Skills (2006) *The Early Years Foundation Stage (EYFS)—consultation on a single quality framework for services to children from birth to five*. Available at: http://www.dfes.gov.uk/. (accessed 8th March 2006).

Dockett, S. and Perry, B. (2001) Starting school: effective transitions. *Early Childhood Research and Practice*, 3(2). Available at: http://ecrp.uiuc.edu/v3n2/dockett.html (accessed 22 August 2002).

Dockett, S. and Perry, B. (2002) Who's ready for what? Young children starting school. *Contemporary Issues in Early Childhood*, 3(1): 67–89.

Dunlop, A-W. (2003) *Mixing Methods in a Study of Transition from Preschool to Primary Education*. London: British Educational Research Association Early Years Special Interest Group, Institute of Education.

Dunlop, A-W. (2004) The challenges of early educational transitions: change the child or change the system? *Proceedings of the Continuity and Change: Educational Transitions International Conference*, Sydney, Australia, EJ. 27 November – 1st December.

Early Years Curriculum Group (1989) *The Early Years Curriculum and the National Curriculum*. Stoke-on-Trent: Trentham Books.

Fabian, H. (2002) *Children Starting School. A Guide to Successful Transitions and Transfers for Teachers and Assistants*. London: David Fulton Publishers.

Fabian, H. and Dunlop, A-W. (eds) (2002) *Transitions in the Early Years. Debating Continuity and Progression for Children in Early Education*. London: RoutledgeFalmer.

Hargreaves, D.H. (2004) *Learning For Life. The Foundations for Lifelong Learning*. Bristol: Policy Press.

Jackson, S (2004) Early childhood policy and services, in T. Maynard and N. Thomas (eds) *An Introduction to Early Childhood Studies*. London: Sage.

Kelly, A.V. (2004) *The Curriculum. Theory and Practice*, 5th edn. London: Sage.

Ladd, G.W. (1990) Having friends, keeping friends, making friends and being liked by peers in the classroom: predictors of children early school adjustment? *Child Development*, 61: 1081–100.

MacNaughton, G. (2003) *Shaping Early Childhood. Learners, Curriculum and Contexts*. Maidenhead: Open University Press.

Margetts, K. (2002) Planning transition programmes, in A-W. Dunlop and H. Fabian (eds) *Transitions in the Early Years. Debating Continuity and Progression for Children in Early Education*. London: RoutledgeFalmer.

McInnes, K. (2002) What are the educational experiences of 4-year-olds? A comparative study of 4-year-olds in nursery and reception settings, *Early Years*, 22(2): 119–27.

Neuman, J. (2002) The wider context: an international overview of transition issues, in A-W. Dunlop and H. Fabian (eds) *Transitions in the Early Years. Debating Continuity and Progression for Children in Early Education*. London: RoutledgeFalmer.

OFSTED (2004) *Transition from the Reception Year to Year 1. An evaluation by HMI*. London: OFSTED.

Parsons, M. and Stephenson, M. (2002) The transition from the Foundation Stage to Key Stage One. Paper presented at the European Early Childhood and Education Research Association Conference, Lefkosia, 28th August 2002.

QCA/Department for Education and Employment (2000) *Curriculum Guidance for the Foundation Stage*. London: QCA.

Welsh National Assembly (2004) *Learning Wales*. Available at: http://

www.learning.wales.gov.uk/scripts/fe/news_details.asp?NEWSID=134 (accessed 6th December 2004).

Wenger, E. (1998) *Communities of Practice: Learning, Meaning and Identity*. Cambridge: Cambridge University Press.

Wood, E. (2004) Developing a pedagogy of play, in A. Anning, J. Cullen and M. Fleer (eds) *Early Childhood Education. Society and Culture*. London: Sage.

Yeboah, D.A. (2002) Enhancing transition from early childhood phase to primary education: evidence from research literature, *Early Years*, 22(1): 51–68.

CONCLUSIONS

11 Bridging research, policy and practice

Aline-Wendy Dunlop

Educational transitions in the early years remain a persistent issue. In this chapter, the main strands of the book are drawn together in a dynamic process, which aims to build on the range of perspectives offered in the different chapters and to contest ideas about the problems of transition by developing a position for using transitions as a tool for change. Descriptions of policies affecting transitions in the countries in which we each work, provided by each author, inform discussion of how policy currently addresses transitions and whether present policy addresses transitions for young children appropriately.

Past work on educational transitions has been dominated by concepts of children's 'school readiness' and of 'school adjustment', both of which are predicated on the idea that it is the child who must change, be resilient, cope with difference and the family who must adapt, rather than question whether school systems themselves should change (Dunlop 2004). At the present time, both these concepts are evident in policy perspectives on transitions in the early years. Tensions exist between, on the one hand, pressures on children to 'be ready' or to adapt to the new demands of the sociocultural context of the school, and on the other, a newer dialogue of the 'ready school' in which there is a growing expectation that settings should be flexible enough to be able to adapt to differences between children and families in any incoming class of children. This chapter sets out to challenge such perspectives and to view transitions not as a problem of readiness or adaptation, but as a tool to be employed to invite new theoretical models, to contest and stimulate policy development and research, as well as to influence the practical day-to-day experience of young children.

The chapter authors have each written extensively on their research into transitions. As the editors, Fabian and Dunlop, have provided the book ends, however these two chapters are more than introductory and concluding. In the opening chapter Fabian identifies the various definitions of transition that, as researchers, we have all used to underpin our research or have developed from our research. In this last chapter, Dunlop's writing focuses on the links between research, policy and practice.

By conceptualizing transitions as a key tool to de-construct our systems, it is proposed that transitions are not only transforming, but need to be transformed. Transitions are a focus (Fabian & Dunlop 2006) in the current Early Childhood Education and Care element of the Education For All (EFA) Global Monitoring Report process (2006), of which the first aim is to expand and improve comprehensive early childhood care and education, especially for the most vulnerable and disadvantaged children. Searching the various uses of the term transition leads us to identify the need for a policy shift, which goes beyond current models of transition. Few countries have any national policy statements about the transition from early childhood provision into school, although it can be argued that the development of curriculum frameworks and guidelines for early childhood is a step towards addressing, protecting and improving early education and care, and making new links to the next stage of education. Although each of our countries are engaged in curriculum change and our country documentation mentions transition to school being of importance, policy for transitions is generally left to the local government level, or to schools to develop and implement, rather than being embraced at national level.

Until the late twentieth century the UK lacked any coherent national policy for early childhood education and care. More recently, current curriculum reform in the different countries of the United Kingdom is being used as a tool to address issues of continuity, progression and pedagogy. In England there is a national strategy for childcare (HM Treasury 2004), which has the ambition of extending the present free entitlement of a nursery education place for 3- and 4-year-olds, so that by 2010 there is an integrated early years service children's centre in every community. At the time of going to press a new consultation document, The Early Years Foundation Stage, has just been released, it is presented as 'a single framework for care, learning and development for children in all early years settings from birth till the August after their 5th birthday' [Department for Education and Skills, (DfES) 2006: i]. In Wales, early years policy has embraced a new concept of early childhood by introducing a curriculum that integrates the foundation stage with the first stage of school in a new foundation phase for children aged 3–7 years: a pilot of their Framework for Children's Learning runs till 2008. In Scotland, a curriculum 3–18 is being developed, with links between early childhood and later schooling being emphasized and a value placed on play as part of early years approaches into the school years. Each of these countries identify curriculum by content areas, even for young children, although the discourse of curriculum documents emphasizes these as areas of development for younger children.

By contrast the Nordic countries aim at development rather than knowledge in their early childhood curricula (Broström & Wagner 2003). Here, too, curriculum guidance, whilst policy-setting, and emphasizing cooperation between 'playschool' and compulsory school, falls short of a national transition policy. Denmark's new curriculum legislation comes closer than most to addressing transitions at national level, a new Act (Socialministeriet 2004) legislating for curriculum in the early years was put forward in the Parliament with three arguments. Curriculum for the early years is aimed to: break down negative social heritage; promote school readiness for all children and equalize differences in educational quality between daycare centres. On a formal level a continuity and progression is established between kindergarten and school. In the act *Faghæfte 25* (Undervisningsministeriet, 2003) the transition is stressed: 'Teaching in kindergarten is aimed towards creating continuity in the children's transition from home and kindergarten to school, but also between kindergarten class and the following classes and after school (leisure time centre)'. These principles are carried through in school documents in most of the Danish municipalities.

Swedish early years policy brings about transitions in different ways. The new preschool classes for 6-year-olds smooth entry to school. Johansson finds that, whilst curriculum states the importance of transitions, policy should be applied across early childhood services, including preschool, preschool class and after-school day-care. Such shared policy would encourage staff exchange of experience, and more integration of the services attended by children. In Denmark and Sweden, as in Iceland curriculum policy emphasizes the intention to encourage the development of the whole child, including the body, movements, emotions, intelligence, language, social development and awareness, appreciation of art and creativity, and moral understanding and awareness. The playschool should take care of all these aspects, strengthen them and encourage their integration. The curriculum states that emphasis should be placed on creative activities and play in playschools. Free and self-initiated play is seen as the most natural form of expression, and the most important way to learn and develop during the playschool years. The curriculum guidelines for playschool and compulsory school represent two different traditions in teaching young children. The primary school guidelines emphasize the teaching of subjects, pupil assessment, and evaluation, but these academic trends have not yet reached the playschool. The differences in playschool and primary school, represented by differences in their guidelines, provide evidence of discontinuity between these two early childhood settings.

In Germany the educational systems as well as the childcare sector are under the authority of the 16 individual regional states (Länder). Despite this diversity there are general themes and developments in early childhood policy in Germany, which include a political debate following criticism in the PISA and OECD reports that budgets for education are too low and that they are seen as costs instead of investment. This debate has led to a new look at the philosophy that underpins early childhood practice, both supply of services and their quality, and day care for children under threes. Early childhood pedagogues' professionalism, education, pay and working conditions are under scrutiny. Quality and accountability in early childhood is answered by the development of early childhood curricula frameworks and assessment measures. Out of 16 conceptualizations of curricula frameworks, four deal with transition from the early childcare sector (German Kindergarten) to compulsory school system from a more comprehensive point of view. The transition research of Griebel and Niesel is informing the most elaborated and theoretically based of these frameworks.

This pattern is repeated in Singapore—a new curriculum framework for kindergartens was introduced in 2003 (Ministry of Education): it focuses on values, skills and attitudes. The curricula for the early stages of school are also being revised to be more in keeping with the more child-centred learning opportunities found in the revised curricular guidelines for kindergarten. At the same time attention is being given to the education of staff and increased liaison between sectors is being encouraged.

Australian policy shows a diversity of practices among the six states and two territories regarding the commencement of schooling. In at least three states, preschools are administered by the school education system, and in the other states/territories preschool services are administered by community welfare or health departments. The compulsory age of entry to school is 6 years. Many state/territory education departments acknowledge that starting school is one of the major challenges of early childhood and strongly influences children's progress at school. Despite this while many states have policies and procedures in place to support the transition of students from primary to secondary school, there are virtually no policies or procedures about transition to primary school. Those that do exist are concerned with the integration of children with disabilities into mainstream primary schooling. The associated literature identifies the aims of integration and the administrative processes, and roles and responsibilities of personal and may provide guidelines for transition. There are no government guidelines or accountability processes about transition practices, and the roles of early childhood, schools and other support services. Rather, it is expected that each early childhood service or school or community will develop their own transition programmes. As a result, some do little or nothing, while others have comprehensive and collaborative transition programs involving a range of stakeholders.

In New Zealand a 10-year strategy for early childhood (Ministry of Education 2002) highlights three aims: to increase participation; to improve the quality of ECE services, and to promote collaborative relationships. This last aim in particular addresses educational provision in what had previously been quite separate systems, despite the focus placed on transitions in the curriculum document *Te Whàriki* (Ministry of Education 1996).

It is important to make opportunities for the young child to experience new challenges, cooperative ventures, and longer term
projects. These experiences also help to meet their expanding capabilities and provide a smooth transition to school. (26)

The 10-year strategy aims for improvement in children's development and
educational achievement to be achieved by collaboration between early
childhood education, school and a range of other providers. Not only is there
an acknowledgement of the importance of different sectors of education relating to each other, but also a relation is made between schools, families,
social services and health (Ministry of Education 2002). At the same time
government use of research evidence is being contested in New Zealand, and
it is asserted that the use of research to legitimize public policy and spending
should be questioned (Farqhuar & Croad 2005: 1). As governments re-
conceptualize educational borders, insights from research into the experience
of various stakeholders in transition to school lead us to question once again
whether it is the interests of children that are at the heart of educational
reform, or whether it is accountability and the mirage of educational outcome, which entices governments to look more closely at the relationships
between early and later stages of education. 'Schools are often perceived to
focus on teaching curriculum content; early childhood programmes on processes of learning' (Cullen 2002, cited in van Dam 2003). This difference of
perspective between systems is common across the globe, but what is new is a
policy concern to bridge those differences. A challenge emerging from the
pages of this book is to use transitions as a tool in that process.

The degree of match or mismatch between the ways in which children
think and learn, and the curricula offered, supports the case for policy change
to focus on transitions practices. By looking at models of transition we can
gauge whether our systems are competent to support children in transition;
by considering how children themselves experience transition, and reflecting
on this from parental and professional viewpoints, we can begin to bridge
from practice through research to policy change.

We have offered an analysis of definitions of transition by addressing
parent, child and practitioner perspectives. Children, parents and teachers are
seen as participative agents in the processes of educational transitions, in the
social groups that surround the child at transition and in the learning
relations that are embedded in transitions. We have worked in our various
studies to include these voices. Sometimes we write from the perspective of
one or other of the agents, but with regard to this dynamic relationship
between all three and the social, cultural and political/policy environments in
which transitions and understandings of transitions are more or less embedded. By considering educational transitions as a relational concept, we can
take account of the multiple transitions that can occur. From these

considerations a better understanding of what is important at transitions can emerge.

If childhood and transitions in childhood are so positioned at the forefront of personal, political and academic agendas, then this chapter must aim to move productively between theory and practice, research and policy, in order to make a contribution towards improving the educational experience of young children. In this way transitions work is a tool through which we can work for children.

The concept of transition

It is time that as researchers in transitions we reconsider our shared understandings of transition as a concept: in the words of one parent 'That's an awful difficult word. Why not just call it starting school?' On one level, the vocabulary of theorizing school start may be guilty of using fancy terms, but at the heart of this lies a view that school start is much more than simply starting school—it is a process of change and, for some, a life-changing experience. This particular childhood change is a common experience across the globe for any child entering institutional or group day care, or education, any child starting elementary education, moving from class to class through the system, or border crossing between countries, across cultural divides (Brooker 2002), and across systems and phases of education. Combined with this, in today's society children may experience multiple changes almost simultaneously. Common as such experiences may be, we cannot assume that they are plain sailing. For some children the winds of change blow fair, for others the passage can be stormy, for others still they drift into the new, and for some they set off on a huge adventure, as explorers in search of something new. It is this very variety of possible experience, including how parents experience their child's transition to school, and the educators working with them, that demand that we work together to support children to maximize the opportunities and learning at times of change.

Almost inevitably the rhetoric of transition to date highlights associated problems: questions of continuity, of whether and when children make progress, of coping with change, of resilience, of changing expectations and new conformities to be absorbed, of adaptation and of whether children are ready for what transition to school may bring. As authors and researchers, we embrace a range of definitions of transitions, but mostly we are writing about change. There is a need to begin to contest if transitions are merely change or if, in fact, they are times of change that bring shifts in culture, identity, role and status, as well as daily experience. If this is the case, then transitions have the capacity to transform both positively and negatively, and further, if they are not always positive, if they are even just a little too challenging for any given child, then the transition itself needs to be transformed.

As evidenced by other work in this field, the interaction between border crossers, and their work and family lives is complex. Historically, research on work and families has adopted several theoretical approaches: an open-systems approach, where researchers (e.g. Katz & Kahn 1978) assumed that events at work influenced events at home and vice-versa. Consideration was also given to the idea that feelings and behaviours could 'spillover' (Staines 1980) from one arena to another (Dunlop 2003a).

Lewin's work talks of 'life-space' (1943), Bourdieu writes of 'habitus' (Bourdieu 1990; Webb et al. 2002) and contends that habitus lies at the core of his methodological framework as he attempts to go beyond and to reconcile such dualisms as 'micro-macro' or agency and structure (Reay 2004). Each implies the need to consider the ways in which new situations and transitions in and out of them influence the individual. Bruner (1990: 95) explains that narrative accounts can explicate a range of views or 'construals' of reality. The stories told of transition into school and of the learning experiences there, may offer insights into how it is for children, their well-being and their learning (Dunlop 2003a).

In looking critically at transitions in childhood we must call into question what we understand by 'childhood'. In considering early childhood transitions, it maybe necessary to embrace the given that all of childhood represents a 'transitional territory between infancy and adulthood in which families have a part and can be social actors and agents' (Fabian & Dunlop 2002: 147). The way in which childhood is conceptualized, for example, as a process of becoming or as valid in itself, will affect how transitions are managed for and by children (Dunlop 2003b). While acknowledging that transitions are normative, we nevertheless assert that they should not be taken for granted.

A model for research into transitions

In writing extensively on our research into transitions, a systems approach based on Bronfenbrenner's ecological theory permeates our work and has provided direction for research approaches. Dunlop's work (2003a) additionally embraces life course theory (Elder 1998, 2001) and this extension allows for acknowledging two things. First, the significance of educational transitions both for children, and for their parents as their own identity and role in relation to their new 'school-child' changes from their previous years of parenting experience. Secondly, in considering the life course we must face our assertions that early educational transitions influence subsequent school success. This is not a given; however, Dunlop also seeks to combine understandings drawn from the educational-sociological perspectives of Bourdieu. Here, the emphasis placed on the place of culture, the importance of habitus and different forms of capital, support the argument that we may carry forward factors influencing our lives in a variety of ways. If little capital accrues to a child at the first transition; subsequently, there may be less to draw on. In education we do not yet give sufficient cognizance to young children's agency (Dunlop 2003b), our concepts of childhood are often influenced by a dominant psychological model—often despite contrary evidence from psychological studies themselves—and by the 'scholarization of childhood' (Mayall 2002), where protection from risks and dangers justifies social exclusion of a minority group: children. The four countries of the UK now have Commissioners for Children and Young People, whose job is about safeguarding and promoting children's rights. One of these rights is to be listened to, and to have your views taken into account (UNICEF 1989, Article 12, UN Convention of the Rights of the Child).

Such definitions and influences on conceptualizing transitions take our collective enterprise in linking our transitions research further than the models of transition identified by Petriwskyj et al.'s review (2005). On the basis of their review of 75 peer-reviewed published articles, including some of our own, transitions are typified in a number of useful ways: as a set of teacher or prior-to-school/school practices, as a time-limited change event, as continuity of experience and as a multi-layered, multi-year process. Our collective thinking embraces each of these representations, but moves beyond all of them. By taking account of Bronfenbrenner, Elder and Bourdieu, as well as the wide range of definitions from our work summarized in Fabian's chapter, we are creating a new discourse of transitions where the layered, linear trajectory, and horizontal and vertical views of transitions are no longer sufficient: we promote a view that transitions are not only complex, but also that they evolve over time, and are dynamic because of the interrelatedness of each of the protagonists, through the relationships between them and the cultures and environments in which they exist. An important focus in our work, and for practice, is therefore consideration of human development in context over time. Ecological systems theory (Bronfenbrenner & Morris 1998) proposes that this consideration, say of children in prior-to-school settings, or in the family, should be influenced by or contrasted with at least two macrosystems. Whilst perhaps eschewing dualisms, we embrace the dual analysis of data: for example in terms of effects such as older/younger, educationally active/passive, participation/control, co-constructed/single shaping, continuity/change. In a Bronfenbrennerian approach this allows us to take account of belief systems, agency-capacity to act, and whether transitions are developing or developmentally instigating. In such a research paradigm we can generate empirical hypotheses with statistical support, which in keeping with Elder and Bronfenbrenner can be explored validly and reliably over time.

Turning to Elder's life course theory (Elder 1998), four defining principles emerge and serve to link parents, teachers and children's life course as each impacts on the other. These four principles are stated as historical time, timing in lives, linked lives and human agency. Elder's concept of historical time, where human beings are not just products, but are producers, sits well with Bronfenbrenner's view of interrelatedness and interaction. Elder states that 'The life course of individuals is embedded in and shaped by the historical times and events they experience over their lifetime' (2001: 183), and also with Bourdieu's concept of habitus: 'A person's individual history is constitutive of habitus, but so also is the whole collective history of family and class that the individual is a member of' (Reay 2004: 434). In terms of timing in lives, the three perspectives allow for change over time (Bronfenbrenner), the impact of transitions or events throughout life being contingent of when they occur in people's lives (Elder's principle of 'timing in lives') and the transforming of individual habitus by the action of, in our case, the school, being the basis for all subsequent experiences (Bourdieu).

Habitus, as a product of early childhood experience, and the consequent individual dispositions, are continually re-structured by an individual's encounters with the outside world (Di Maggio 1979, cited in Reay 2004). Part of these encounters are relationships with others, what Elder calls 'linked lives', where he envisages that 'lives are lived interdependently and social and historical influences are expressed through this network of shared relationships'. Bronfenbrenner on the other hand considers the 'differential impact of historical events and role transitions on different members of the same family experiencing these same events and transitions' (Bronfenbrenner & Morris 1998: 1021). From these different vantage points, perspectives may well diverge.

All three theorists identify human agency as critical. For Elder 'individuals construct their own life course through choices and actions they take within the opportunities and constraints of history and social circumstances' (2001: 184). Bronfenbrenner highlights the interrelatedness of human experience in which context plays a huge part. This social construction of experience on his model still allows space for individual action, and this seems to emerge in Bourdieu's work too, where we find dispositions are embedded in, or at least reflective of the social context in which they are developed (Reay 2004:), but where social reality and social agency complement. When individual habitus or disposition encounters a field with which it is not familiar, change and transformation occur, for children may become like a 'fish out of water'. This contrasts powerfully with 'social reality exists, so to speak, twice, in things and in minds, in field and in habitus, outside and inside social agents. And when habitus encounters a social world of which it is the product, it is like a 'fish in water': it does not feel the weight of the water and it takes the world about itself for granted' (Bourdieu & Wacquant 1992: 127).

This interweaving of interaction, change and time recognizes the over-lapping layers of children's experience, and the possibility of a dynamic interrelationship between home, early childhood settings and school. This dynamic relationship is mirrored by the interrelationship of research, practice and policy as proposed here as an essential way forward.

Policy

In teasing out what we mean by policy, several levels are recognized. Research has a place at each of the levels we now describe. Policy is enacted at school, local, regional and national levels. At each level efforts are made to respond to over-arching policy developments at a national level. Sometimes the policy impetus has its source within a particular school, cluster of schools or locality, sometimes the influence to change practice is external, driven by national or regional developments. The vocabulary also shifts, for example, 'policy' is deemed to carry obligation and also resource implications; 'strategy' is softer and often used as a developmental model where aspiration to develop policy is present; 'guidelines' tends to be used when a policy direction is sought, but the total climate for a positive reception for a given policy is absent and so guidelines are seen as a way forward, allowing practical approaches through which there is a hope to bring about change to be supported. In some countries policy brings inspection of practice as a vehicle to force change, strategy invites participation, and guidelines provide support and bench-marks, but leave scope for local decision making.

As researchers of transitions, we have had and do presently have an involvement in policy development. The applied nature of our work implies a desire to effect change in practice, based on researching practice, analysing data, and arriving at a position where insights can be drawn out and applied from the research. If this 'virtuous cycle' of research and practice is to be long lasting or widely effective, it needs to move into the policy arena. Where research is commissioned by policy makers this is an expected relationship. Such steering of educational research can alter the nature of knowledge production as it leads to particular forms of evidence: generally for policy performance measurement and management. The relationship between research and policy at Government level is therefore a significant one: the direction of influence should be interrogated.

Our own research in this field is strongly practice based, rather than policy driven, but we now need to ask the question: 'To what extent has transition research been policy steering research?' In several of our countries there is growing evidence of transition emerging as an issue. Our particular research grouping in early childhood is also expanding its work in order to consider other transitions, for example, the links between early childhood transitions and the transition to secondary school (Dunlop 2005a,b), transitions to Higher Education (Fabian & Williams, in preparation), transitions for parents (Dockett & Perry 2005; Dunlop 2005a,b), parental influence in curriculum reform and local governance (Johansson 2002), and the democratic development of transition guidelines (Dunlop & Fabian 2006; Nicholson 2006).

Practice

In practice, children's pathway into school from prior-to-school settings may be affected by existing links between systems: countries with tightly connected links between preschool and primary will at the very least guarantee some form of induction into school, and where there is a nationally standardized curriculum, institutionally based pathways into school can be identified, whereas in countries where the coupling between prior-to-school settings and school is loose, children may experience more individually constructed pathways at transition. The chapters in this book give many insights into practice, and a range of transition practices and issues are well represented. The task here is to link the knowledge of practice generated by our research to policy development. Two policy development projects—both finally settling for 'guidelines' as their title, are informative in the process of linking research, practice and policy development (Dunlop 2002a,b,c; Dunlop & Fabian 2006). Their strength lies in adopting a democratic model for change, with practitioners contributing to and taking responsibility for policy development (Dunlop 2006; Fabian 2006).

An investigation into transitions practice (Dunlop 2002a,b,c) for one local authority in Scotland provides a set of themes, which policy may need to address and on which practice guidelines could be based. They include:

- The contribution of early years nursery education.
- The contribution of early years primary education.
- The contribution of parents.
- Being a home child, being a preschool child, becoming a school child—changing identities.
- Knowing about the new setting and ways of finding out.
- Knowing about the people in the new setting.
- What will school be like? The nature of learning in each setting.
- What is the curriculum like? An appropriate curriculum.
- Well trained staff.
- Partnership with parents.
- Liaison.
- Starting points.

The transitions children make into group day-care, early years nursery settings, primary education, after-school care and other community settings, and on through the primary years and into secondary education can have an impact on the whole family. As children and young people move through their education, they assume new roles and responsibilities, form new relationships and attune to new situations. These shifts mean that they are likely to be seen differently by those around them, and this will bring associated transitions for the family, the school and the community as well.

There are also non-educational transitions that children make, which will affect their passage through life and therefore through school. Family developmental processes bring a range of transitions; for example:

- in family composition;
- through parenthood;
- moving to new neighbourhoods;
- through separation or divorce;
- in relationships within families and in employment status.

These are just some of the family-life transitions that occur. The school can play an important role in both educational and non-educational transitions for children (Dunlop 2002c). Guidance on transitions aims to support practitioners to bridge research and practice, and can promote strong links between early childhood services and children's future experiences (Stirling Council Children's Services 2005).

In-service sessions focusing on play as a bridge from preschool to primary school, in another Scottish local authority, led to a current project to develop transition guidelines. Here, the approach has been based on an inclusive model of policy development, in which an equally divided group of around 100 preschool and primary staff responded to a survey, became involved in practice workshops led by the researchers, and introduced a new transition focus to their practice. A set of guidelines have been developed based on the analysis of the survey, which allowed strengths and gaps in practice to be identified. Practitioners shared their current work, providing examples from practice to enrich the guidance (Dunlop & Fabian 2006). Examples included combined events for prior-to-school and school children; a buddy system where older children supported younger ones throughout the school day and, in particular, in the playground and at mealtimes; good liaison between nursery and primary teachers; school visits and tours; a video of the new school 'through the eyes of a child'; nursery children joining in class with last year's leavers; photo records of school visits; training for buddies; home visits; staff discussions and closer links between settings to ease children's transitions.

Reflections

Fabian has defined transitions in Chapter 1 as 'a complex process made up of continued social activity in which the individual lives, and learns to cope, by adapting to the given social conditions'. She reflects on what this means for educational practice, in the light of a separate set of social and cognitive demands (Dunlop & Fabian 2002). A range of policies can be seen to have prompted improvements in transitions: Sure Start in the UK, the Ten Year Strategy in NZ, OECD Starting Strong (2001) across Europe, curriculum change, development and reform in many countries. Through research those involved in the transition to school can be influential in bringing about change. In this context of broad policy influence and research, some key questions arise:

- Can policy better support and empower children in transition?
- Is it essential that parents, educators, policy makers and politicians pay close attention to young children's early transitions?
- Given the rights of children to express a view and to be heard in all matters that affect them, in relation to age and maturity, how can we meet these obligations and ensure such consultation around educational transitions?
- How does research inform policy and practice of early education transitions for young children?
- What is the potential impact of research and policy on transition practice?
- Can we generate a new model of transition practice by drawing on research, policy and practice?

Bridging the gap between research, policy and practice

A desire to bridge research, policy and practice is an effort in triangulation. Through practice, research and policy engagement a new way of tackling early childhood transitions may evolve. Research efforts specific to early childhood transition are growing; they are matched by research that focuses on the transfer to secondary school, and into higher education or the workplace. Attention is brought to the particular challenges of effective transition for able pupils, for people with additional needs, for adolescents, familialy, and in lifestyle and health. This growing field has reached a stage when it is important to integrate such efforts in order to contest transitions in people's lives.

Openness to change and vulnerability to the effects of change are features of transitional periods. The knowledge base developed by research into transitions provides the evidence needed in order to respond to and address issues of children's social exclusion, and improve well-being. Consideration of transition practice and monitoring of outcomes in transition programmes could begin to address the need for structural change—according to country patterns of loosely coupled preschool/tightly connected links, and could focus on the training needs of staff. By involving stakeholders in research, as described in this book, we can ensure their voices reach forward into policy development. In this way, children's perspectives, action research by practitioners with children and parental perspectives can contribute to political problem solving. Research can provide this necessary link between practice and policy, should be able to guarantee reliable evidence and, in return, close the loop through dissemination in locally impacting guidelines on practice and policy for children. Thus, a framework for action can be developed and children's services may be influenced positively.

Conclusions

In this chapter transitions have been promoted as a new field of enquiry and 'transitions capital' as a tool for policy change. A new vocabulary of transitions is emerging, but we have to be careful that this vocabulary of transitions avoids glossing over crucial issues that will begin to transform the scholarization of transitions into a model that takes account of the interrelatedness of domains children inhabit and wider society. The idea of co-constructing transitions developed and used by Griebel and Neisel, that espouses the heterogeneity of any school entrant group, suggests that a next step is towards co-constructing policy. Structures, identity and agency, liveable lives, lived lives, identified strategies that claim to be teachable such as resilience and other forms of social competence; capacity building, mobility and unsettlement, and learning trajectories, if glossed become 'weasel words': no-one can afford to gloss such a complex area of study, of policy and of practice. By creating a culture of listening to children, to the adults who love and care for them, and to the professionals who work for them, it may be possible in the never-ending encoding process of policy (Ball 1994) to generate a strong forum for linking research, practice and policy enactment to the politicized world of policy formulation.

If these two sets of early childhood experience are well linked by successful transition from the one to the other, and not simply for a short settling-in period, but over time, through curriculum, pedagogical practice, relationships, good communication, listening to each other and to children, then the long-term effects claimed for early childhood programmes will be supported by successful transitions, which will set children up to do well and are likely to avoid longer-term dips in children's learning, will promote continuity where appropriate, and capacities and dispositions to deal with change where it, too, is beneficial. Transitions research will then be able to move forward from problematizing transitions, to demonstrating that successful transitions are a positive tool for change.

The two worlds of preschool and school are both important, and have identities that should not be lost, the bridge between them is important, a recognizable landscape on each side of the gap helps, but the ability to do well has to be rooted in successful transition. It also needs to be recognized that personal targets for progress and policy targets for progression may be different, and consequently what is seen as success in transition may be variable, according to the stakeholder.

The notion of successful transition now needs further exploration. Here, over-simplification should be avoided. There are many ways to define transitions and many perspectives on what makes a successful transition, for example, the lifelong may be more important than the immediate transfer. Multiple indicators are needed, including social and cultural literacy, attention to context and environment, respect for and inclusion of the range of stakeholders, extended timeframes to allow for individual and system difference, acknowledgement of the importance of a concept of transition, providing continuities but not sameness, maintaining distinctive and appropriate education for young children, as is their right.

A new model emerging from this discussion is 'Transitions Capital'. As researchers we are passionately engaged in generating solutions to the challenge of early childhood transitions, which is different from 'steered' work. In a sense, therefore, our research is small scale: passion tends to be intimate, focused and intense. Where our work is larger scale, it tends to focus down on a smaller number of children, teachers or parents in order to hear their voice. Depth can be argued both to be narrowed or to bring wisdom: for us, the passion and the depth is part of our transitions habitus, our dispositions in our work, which is, in itself, generative: we are at a stage in our shared enterprise where there is an active effect of knowledge on itself: this is more than knowledge transfer.

This new notion of 'transitions capital' as an essential part of influencing the field, the expectation of creating a field of enquiry that embraces the many transitions that affect our lives, and the possibility of transitions being both transformed and a tool for transforming policy, research and practice, is an exciting one.

References

Ball, S.J. (1994) *Education Reform. A Critical and Post-structural Approach.* Buckingham: Open University Press.

Bourdieu, P. (1990) *The Logic of Practice.* Cambridge: Polity Press.

Bourdieu, P. & Waquant, L. (1992) *An Invitation to Reflexive Sociology*. Chicago: University of Chicago Press.

Bronfenbrenner, U. & Morris, P. (1998) The ecology of developmental processes, in R.M. Lerner (ed.) *The Handbook of Child Psychology: Theoretical Models of Human Development*, Vol. 1, 5th edn. New York: Wiley & Sons.

Broström, S. & Wagner, J.T. (eds) (2003) *Early Childhood Education in Five Nordic Countries: Perspectives on the Transition from Preschool to School*. Århus: Systime Academic.

Brooker, L. (2002) Starting School – Young Children Learning Cultures. Buckingham Open University Press.

Bruner, J.S. (1990) *Acts of Meaning*. Cambridge: Harvard University Press.

Cullen, J. (1998) Emergent learners: making the transition to school learning, *Childrens Issues*, 2(1): 30–3.

Department for Education and Skills (2006) *The Early Years Foundation Stage (EYFS)—Consultation on a Single Quality Framework for Services to Children from Birth to Five*. http://www.dfes.gov.uk/ accessed 08.05.06.

Di Maggio, P. (1979) Review essay: 'On Pierre Bourdieu', *American Journal of Sociology* 84(6): 1460–74.

Dockett, S., & Perry, B. (2003) Smoothing the way: what makes a successful school transition program? *Education Links*, 65: 6–10.

Dockett, S. and Perry, B. (2005) Family issues and expectations as children start school. Paper presented at the EECERA 15th Annual Conference, Dublin, Ireland 31 August – 3 September 2005.

Dunlop, A.W.A. (2002a) *Research Literature Review. Early Years Educational Transitions. Working Together for Children in the Early Years. Liaison Continuity and Progression from Nursery to Primary Education: Stirling Council*. Glasgow: University of Strathclyde.

Dunlop, A.W.A. (2002b) *Researching Current Transition Practice in Stirling Council 2001 and 2002. Early Years Educational Transitions. Working Together for Children in the Early Years. Liaison Continuity and Progression from Nursery to Primary Education: Stirling Council*. Glasgow: University of Strathclyde.

Dunlop, A.W.A. (2002c) *Guidelines for Action. Early Years Educational Transitions. Working Together for Children in the Early Years. Liaison Continuity and Progression from Nursery to Primary Education: Stirling Council*. Glasgow: University of Strathclyde.

Dunlop, A.W.A. (2003a) *Transitions and Coping with Change: Status, Identity & Confidence: Key Elements of Change on Transition to School*. Keynote, BPS Conference: Psychology of Education Section, 8th November 2003, Birmingham.

Dunlop, A-W. (2003b) Bridging early educational transitions in learning through children's agency, *Transitions. European Early Childhood Education Research Journal*, Themed Monograph Series, 1: 67–86.

Dunlop, A-W. (2004) The challenges of early educational transitions: change the child or change the system? in D. Whitton, B. Perry & S. Dockett (eds) *Continuity and Change; Transitions in Education*, Conference proceedings, 27–28 November. Sydney: University of Western Sydney.

Dunlop, A-W.A. (2005a) 'I'd like to be a fly on the wall': how does children's transition to school affect parents? Presentation at EECERA 15th Annual Conference, Dublin, 31 August–3 September.

Dunlop, A-W.A. (2005b) 'Don't give yourself a reputation': accessing the views of secondary school entrants. SERA Annual Conference, Perth, 24–26 November.

Dunlop, A-W.A. (2006) A democratic process—symposium paper 1, in A-W.A. Dunlop, H. Fabian & K. Nicholson (eds) *Transitions Policy Development as a Democratic Process*, European Early Childhood Education Research Association Annual Conference, Iceland, 30 August–2 September.

Dunlop, A-W.A. & Fabian, H. (2006) A democratic development: guidelines for the transitions from preschool to school. Article based on EECERA 2006 symposium (unpublished paper).

Elder, G.H. Jnr (1998) The life course and human development, in R. M. Lerner (ed.) *Handbook of Child Psychology, Volume 1: Theoretical Models of Human Development*, 5th edn. New York: Wiley.

Elder, G.H. Jnr (2001) Families, social change, and individual lives, *Marriage & Family Review*. 177–192 Haworth Press.

Fabian, H. (2006) Creating a new culture, Symposium paper 2, in A-W.A. Dunlop, H. Fabian & K. Nicholson, *Transitions Policy Development as a Democratic Process*, European Early Childhood Education Research Association Annual Conference, Iceland, 30 August–2 September.

Fabian, H. and Dunlop, A-W. (2002) *Inter-conneXions, Early Years Matters*. Dundee: Learning and Teaching Scotland: 3.

Fabian, H. & Dunlop, A-W.A. (2006) Outcomes of Good Practice in Transition Processes for Children Entering Primary School. Paper commissioned by the van Leer foundation as evidence for their response to the EFA Global Monitoring Report 2007.

Fabian, H. and Williams, G. K. (in preparation) 'The Transition to Higher Education: Choice and Influence'.

Farquhar, S. & Croad, G. (2005) *The Competent Children Research: A Flagship for Public Policy and Spending in Early Childhood Education and Care?* Porirua, New Zealand: Childforum Research Network.

HM Treasury ((2004) *Choice for Parents, the Best Start for Children: a Ten Year Strategy for Childcare*. London: Stationery Office.

Johansson, I. (2002) Parents' views of transition to school and their influences in this process, in H. Fabian & A-W. Dunlop (eds) *Transitions in the Early Years, Debating Continuity and Progression in Early Education*. London: RoutledgeFalmer.

Katz, D. and Kahn, R. L. (1978) *The Social Psychology of Organizations*. New York: Wiley.

Lewin, K. (1943) Psychology and the process of group living, *Journal of Social Psychology*, 17: 113–31.

Mayall, B. (2002) *Towards a Sociology for Childhood: Thinking from Children's Lives*. Buckingham: Open University Press.

Ministry of Education (1996) *Te Whàriki Early Childhood Curriculum*. Wellington: MOE.

Ministry of Education (2002) *Pathways to the future: Ngä Huarahi Arataki*. Wellington: MOE. Available at: <www.minedu.govt.nz>. Accessed 25 April 2006.

OECD (2001) *Starting Strong. Early Childhood Education and Care*. Paris: Organization for Economic Cooperation and Development.

Petriwskyj, A., Thorpe, K. & Taylor, C. (2005). Trends in construction of transition to school in three western regions, 1990–2004, *International Journal of Early Years Education*, 13(1): 55–69.

Reay, D. (2004) 'It's all becoming a habitus': beyond the habitual use of habitus in educational research, *British Journal of Sociology of Education*, 25(4): 431–44.

Socialministeriet (2004) *Bekendtgørelse om temaer og mål I pædagogiske læreplaner*. København: Socialministeriet.

Undervisningsministeriet (2003) *Fælles Mål, Faghæfte 25, Børnehaveklassen*, Uddannelsesstyrelsens håndbogsserie nr. 12. Undervisningsministeriet.

Staines, G.L. (1980) Spillover versus compensation: a review of the literature on the relationship between work and non-work, *Human Relations*, 33: 11–129.

Stirling Council Children's Services (2005) *Supporting Transitions. Guidelines to Support Effective Transitions from Nursery to Primary*. Stirling: Stirling Council.

UNICEF (1989) *UN Convention on the Rights of the Child*. Available at: http://www.unicef.org/crc/ (accessed April 25 2006).

UNESCO (2006) *Education for All Global Monitoring Report*. Available at: http://portal.unesco.org/education/ (accessed 25 April 2006).

van Dam, D. (2003) *A submission to the Ministry of Education in Response to the Ten-year Strategic Plan Policy Document, Pathways to the future: Ngä Huarahi Arataki*. Otago: University of Otago, Children's Issues Centre.

Webb, J., Schirato, T. & Danaher, G. (2002) *Understanding Bourdieu*. London: Sage Publications.

Index